Document-Based Assessment Activities for Global History Classes

Theresa C. Noonan

J. WESTON
WALCH
PUBLISHER

Portland, Maine

User's Guide
to
Walch Reproducible Books

As part of our general effort to provide educational materials that are as practical and economical as possible, we have designated this publication a "reproducible book." The designation means that purchase of the book includes purchase of the right to limited reproduction of all pages on which this symbol appears:

Here is the basic Walch policy: We grant to individual purchasers of this book the right to make sufficient copies of reproducible pages for use by all students of a single teacher. This permission is limited to a single teacher and does not apply to entire schools or school systems, so institutions purchasing the book should pass the permission on to a single teacher. Copying of the book or its parts for resale is prohibited.

Any questions regarding this policy or requests to purchase further reproduction rights should be addressed to:

Permissions Editor
J. Weston Walch, Publisher
321 Valley Street • P. O. Box 658
Portland, Maine 04104-0658

1   2   3   4   5   6   7   8   9   10
ISBN 0-8251-3874-4

Contents

Introduction

Robin W. Winks, in *The Historian As Detective*, makes the analogy between the works of two professions—the historian and the detective. It is a link that we want students to make as we ask them to "do history." Just as historians become detectives as they work with clues from the past, students should learn to examine evidence, question its relevance, assess its validity, and then formulate hypotheses which they test further. Often these answers are challenged by others as they interpret the evidence and arrive at conflicting interpretations. Being a historical detective is challenging, engaging, exciting work.

This book is designed to help teachers and students become better historians, thinkers, and writers. It provides them with opportunities to do the work of all three at one time. They examine evidence and data in order to arrive at informed and thoughtful positions, then present their thoughts clearly, logically, and effectively in writing. Although this is a challenging task, the required skills can be developed with practice—skills that we all need in order to be effective citizens and lifelong learners.

What Is a Document-Based Question, or DBQ?

A **document-based question** is a writing task in which a student analyzes significant evidence—documents and other data—to reach an informed position, then presents that information in a persuative, logical, and accurate essay. The questions are generally open-ended, giving students the opportunity to develop responses to the questions using the documents and the information they have learned in their study of global history. The documents are mostly primary sources or eyewitness accounts provided by people who were actually "making history" or witnessing the events being examined. These primary sources include diaries, speeches, newspaper accounts, reports, and cartoons. Other documents considered primary sources are maps, photos, graphs, and charts. In addition, secondary accounts or later interpretations of the events are included to provide different perspectives. Secondary accounts are written by people who have studied the primary sources and reached conclusions based on the evidence. At times these conclusions are contested by others who present conflicting interpretations, making for interesting analysis. Just as two eyewitnesses can disagree about what happened, historians also disagree and offer different interpretations as to what happened and why it happened. Both provide raw material for historians.

Why Use DBQ's?

Document-based questions require students to think analytically when using the documents, and to write responses that integrate information from a variety of sources. These are very important skills. Some of the skills involved in historical analysis include:

- evaluating the reliability, validity, and accuracy of historical sources
- identifying the point of view of these sources as well as determining bias
- identifying a problem or issue and considering alternative positions and solutions
- categorizing information as political, social, or economic, or as positive or negative
- comparing and contrasting different interpretations of key events
- constructing support for a position by choosing accurate, relevant evidence

Writing skills are crucial. Students need a process in place for addressing document-based questions. They need direct instruction using primary sources and conflicting interpretations of historical events, as well as repeated opportunities to practice these skills in class and in independent practice or homework. The students should be engaged in analyzing documents and writing in conjunction with documents almost daily. The questions provided in this book can be used as a basis for class discussion or as preparation for a debate or seminar. They can be used for research projects or in extended writing tasks, as well as for formal assessment. These questions could also be used in an essay portion of a unit or final exam. If used as part of an assessment, it is important that students understand the expectations of this type of writing. Consequently, they must be familiar with the rubric that defines the criteria or characteristics of the content and skills required for each level of performance. A generic rubric has been included in this book (on page *vii*); however, it should be tailored to specific questions. In addition, students benefit most if English and social studies teachers use a common vocabulary and integrate instruction to reinforce the appropriate thinking and writing skills in both classes. Students and teachers need to examine exemplary or "anchor" papers and to reflect on their own development of writing skills. For that reason, student responses to several questions have been included in this book and can be used for instructional purposes. All students need to be effective thinkers and writers. Consequently, instructional strategies that develop these skills are important parts of every teacher's repertoire.

How to Use and Teach DBQ's

The document-based questions in this book are suitable for use with high-school students and can be used in a variety of ways as described above. They may also be used with more able upper middle-school students who have been given enough practice with this format. Students usually have experience working with documents throughout their educational careers. Students in primary and intermediate grades work with age-appropriate artifacts, diaries, maps, and documents of all kinds. Consequently, when teachers at the middle- or high-school level engage students with these kinds of sources, they need to remind students that they have had plenty of experience in "doing history" with documents. The documents in this book may be complex or lengthy, but students *can* do this type of thinking and writing. Because of the lack of experience of some students, teachers may want to further edit some of the documents or limit the number of documents they choose to use. In the beginning, it is best to introduce the documents in this book as part of class instruction, so that the analytical skills can be taught directly or practiced in a supported environment. Each of the DBQ's includes scaffolding in the form of questions that guide the student in interpreting the documents and in addressing the main question or prompt. To help students develop these skills, teachers can use the documents as part of instruction on a particular topic. For example, the DBQ on ancient Greece, as well as pictures of representative art and architecture, can be used in daily lessons before it is used as a culminating unit essay test question. To assist the teacher, in addition to the documents with scaffolding, each DBQ is followed by a grading key. Several DBQ's also include a ninth-grade student's work and teacher assigned grades and comments. In addition, a Guide to Responding to Document-Based Questions has been included for students because it is important for them to have a process to use when addressing DBQ's. With the guide, the rubric, the documents, the model student work, and the suggestions for instruction provided in this book you are equipped to teach students how to write effective essays using documents.

To the Student

The **document-based questions** in this book are designed to help you become a skillful historian and a competent writer. Examining real evidence about important questions in history and weighing evidence against what you already know in order to reach a position reflect what historians do. These skills are authentic to the analysis of history. Using primary source documents, conflicting interpretations of historical events, interpreting graphs, cartoons, maps, charts, then constructing an understanding of an event or era are important skills for everyone to possess and to demonstrate. Writing answers to DBQ's will help you improve your complex reasoning skills, to learn to detect bias, to weigh evidence, to develop logical solutions, and to express yourself in a clear, thoughtful, persuasive essay. The Guide to Responding to Document-Based Questions included in the book provides you with a process to use whenever you are writing a DBQ essay. If you also want to know how your essay will be evaluated, the Scoring Rubric identifies the criteria used in grading your DBQ essay. Use this rubric to grade your essays before handing them to your teacher. In addition, ask your teacher to duplicate an exemplar essay from this book or from your class so you can clearly see a model essay. You are now ready to begin. Start by reviewing the Guide to Responding to Document-Based Questions and the Scoring Rubric.

Guide to Responding to Document-Based Questions

A DBQ provides you with an opportunity to weigh significant evidence/documents to reach an informed position and to present the information in response to a question.

Process

1. **Read the question carefully.** What does the question ask you to do? Underline key words, eras, names, issues, or categories used in the question.
2. **Write down the facts**—names, dates, events—that you know about the topic and time period.
3. **Read and analyze the documents:**
   - Look at the author and the time the document was written.
   - Identify the point of view or main idea of the document. Underline key words. Write notes in the margin summarizing each document.
   - Respond to the prompt questions after the document. If there are no questions, write down the main ideas.
4. **Reread the question.** Carefully consider your document summaries and their relationship to the question asked.
5. **Plan/organize your response so that you prove your thesis with supporting evidence and information (categorize, block, outline, mind map).**
   - Identify the main subjects to be discussed in the body.
   - Select the documents related to each major subject.
   - Write down important information from the documents and from your knowledge of the issue.
6. **Write an organized essay responding to the question.**
   - <u>Introductory paragraph</u>. Take a stand on the question. Respond to all parts of the question. Develop your thesis. To what degree is it true? Provide background and explanation and definition of terms used in the question. Introduce the topics you will discuss in the body of your essay.
   - <u>Body paragraphs</u>. Use a separate paragraph for each topic, issue, or argument. Include specific examples to support generalizations or to make distinctions. Cite specific evidence from the documents but avoid long quotations. Integrate information from the documents and from your knowledge in responding to the questions.
   - <u>Concluding paragraph</u>. Restate your position and main ideas that you presented in your essay.

Generic Scoring Rubric*

5
- Thoroughly addresses all aspects of the task by accurately analyzing and interpreting most of the documents
- Incorporates relevant outside information
- Richly supports essay with relevant facts, examples, and details
- Writes a well-developed essay, consistently demonstrating a logical and clear plan of organization
- Uses information from the documents in the body of the essay, but does not copy document
- Includes a strong introduction and conclusion

4
- Addresses all aspects of the task by accurately analyzing and interpreting most of the documents
- Incorporates relevant outside information
- Includes relevant facts, examples, and details, but discussion may be more descriptive than analytical
- Writes a well-developed essay, demonstrating a logical and clear plan of organization
- Includes a good introduction and conclusion

3
- Addresses most aspects of the task or addresses all aspects in a limited way; uses some of the documents
- Incorporates limited or no relevant outside information
- Uses some facts, examples, and details, but discussion is more descriptive than analytical
- Writes a satisfactorily developed essay, demonstrating a general plan of organization
- Restates the theme in the introduction and concludes with a simple restatement of the theme

2
- Attempts to address some aspects of the task, making limited use of the documents
- No relevant outside information
- Presents few facts, examples, and details; simply restates contents of the documents
- Writes a poorly organized essay, lacking focus
- Has vague or missing introduction and/or conclusion

1
- Shows limited understanding of the task with vague, unclear references to the documents
- Presents no relevant outside information
- Attempts to complete the task, but essay demonstrates a major weakness in organization
- Uses little or no accurate or relevant facts, details, or examples
- Has vague or missing introduction and/or conclusion

0
- Fails to address the task
- Is illegible
- Blank paper

* Provided by the New York State Education Department

Name_____ Date_____

DBQ 1: Ancient Greek Contributions

Historical Context:

Many of the roots of Western civilization can be traced back to the ancient Greeks. They made long-lasting contributions in the areas of art, architecture, philosophy, math, drama, and science.

◆ **Directions:** The following question is based on the accompanying documents in Part A. As you analyze the documents, take into account both the source of the document and the author's point of view. Be sure to:

1. Carefully read the document-based question. Consider what you already know about this topic. How would you answer the question if you had no documents to examine?

2. Now, read each document carefully, underlining key phrases and words that address the document-based question. You may also wish to use the margin to make brief notes. Answer the questions which follow each document.

3. Based on your own knowledge and on the information found in the documents, formulate a thesis that directly answers the question.

4. Organize supportive and relevant information into a brief outline.

5. Write a well-organized essay proving your thesis. The essay should be logically presented and should include information both from the documents and from your own knowledge outside of the documents.

> **Question:** *What were the contributions to Western civilization from the ancient Greeks?*

◆ **Part A:** The following documents will help you understand the contributions of the ancient Greeks. Examine each document carefully, and answer the question or questions that follow.

Document 1

This quotation is from Socrates, who lived from about 470 to about 399 B.C.

> The unexamined life is not worth living.

Who was Socrates, and what was he suggesting in this quote? _____

_____

_____

_____

(continued)

*Document-Based Assessment
Activities for Global History Classes*

DBQ 1: Ancient Greek Contributions *(continued)*

Document 2

This quotation is from Aristotle, who lived in Greece from 384 to 322 B.C.

> Since human reason is the most godlike part of human nature, a life guided by human reason is superior to any other. . . . For man, this is the life of reason, since the faculty of reason is the distinguishing characteristic of human beings.

Who was Aristotle, and what did he believe about human nature? _____

_____

_____

Document 3

This excerpt is from Pericles' Funeral Oration, given to the Athenians in about 430 B.C.

> Our plan of government favors the many instead of the few:
> that is why it is called a democracy. . . .
> As for social standing, advancement is open to everyone, according to ability. While every citizen
> has an equal opportunity to serve the public, we reward our most distinguished citizens
> by asking them to make our political decisions. Nor do we discriminate against the poor.
> A man may serve his country no matter how low his position on the social scale.

What type of government was Pericles describing? What were his expectations for citizens in

this type of government? _____

_____

_____

Document 4

Following is an excerpt from the Hippocratic oath. Hippocrates, creator of this oath, lived from about 460 to about 377 B.C.

> I will follow that [treatment] which, according to my ability and judgment, I will
> consider for the benefit of my patients, and abstain from whatever is [harmful].
> I will give no deadly medicine to anyone if asked, nor suggest any such [advice] . . .

Who was Hippocrates, and what was he promising to do? _____

_____

_____

(continued)

DBQ 1: Ancient Greek Contributions *(continued)*

Document 5

This excerpt is from the *Elements*, written by Euclid in about 300 B.C.

> Proposition 15, THEOREM: If two straight lines cut one another,
> the vertical, or opposite, angles shall be equal.

Who was Euclid, and what has been the impact of his work? _____

_____

Document 6

This is an excerpt from the play *Antigone* by Sophocles, written in about 441 B.C. In this play, Antigone defies the king's order and buries her brother, who was killed while leading a rebellion.

> *Creon:* And still you dared to overstep these laws?
>
> *Antigone:* For me, it was not Zeus who made that order. Nor do I think your orders were so strong that you, a mortal man, could overrun the gods' unwritten and unfailing laws. . . . I know I must die . . . but if I left my brother dead and unburied, I'd have cause to grieve as now I grieve not.

What values are expressed in this Greek play? _____

_____

Document 7

The Parthenon

How have specific features of this building influenced Western civilization? _____

_____

_____

(continued)

*Document-Based Assessment
Activities for Global History Classes*

Name_____ Date_____

Document 8

Myron's famous marble sculpture of *The Discus Thrower (Diskobolus)* represents an Olympic event.

What does this statue reveal about Greek values? _____

_____

How did the Olympics influence later civilizations? _____

_____

◆ **Part B—Essay**

> *What were the contributions to Western civilization from the ancient Greeks?*

Grading Key

Document 1

Socrates was a philosopher from Athens who believed that a person must ask questions and seek to understand life.

Document 2

Aristotle was also a philosopher. He believed that reason is what makes man "superior" to other living things. Reason makes human beings unique.

Document 3

Pericles was describing a democracy where everyone had an equal opportunity to advance and to serve their country. However, everyone was also expected to participate in civic affairs regardless of their social position.

Document 4

Hippocrates was a Greek doctor who promised that he would provide only medical care that helped his patients. This indicates the responsibility placed on doctors which continues to today.

Document 5

Euclid was a Greek mathematician. His ideas were the basis for the field of geometry, which is studied around the world today.

Document 6

This drama is an example of the important role that the gods played in Greek life. Antigone felt she had to obey her conscience rather than the laws of mortal men.

Document 7

The Parthenon has the columns and pediment that characterize Greek architecture. The balance and simplicity of lines are evident in government buildings around the world, particularly in the West.

Document 8

This marble statue of the *Discobolus* is evidence of the Greek interest in a perfect human body. It also shows the Greek interest in physical activities and skills, which were demonstrated in Olympic competition.

Additional Information Beyond the Documents

The documents in this DBQ provide students with only fragments of evidence. Their answers and essays should include relevant information beyond just the documents—information that students have learned from their classroom study, outside reading and viewing, and other supplemental activities. The following list suggests some of the concepts, people, and events that students might include in their essays from their outside learning.

Knowledge of additional individuals such as Plato, Aristotle, and Homer, and contributions in the areas of:
- drama
- poetry
- historical writing
- architecture
- sculpture
- philosophy
- mathematics
- science

Philosophy:
- Socrates
- Plato
- Aristotle

Drama: Tragedies
- Sophocles—*Oedipus Rex, Antigone*
- Euripides
- Aeschylus

Mythology

Olympic Games

Democracy:
- Athens—Pericles
- Sparta

Architecture:
- Parthenon
- columns on Acropolis

Math and Science:
- Euclid—geometry
- Archimedes
- Hippocrates

Name_____ Date_____

DBQ 2: Fall of the Western Roman Empire

Historical Context:

In the third century A.D. Rome faced many problems. In addition to internal decay, the invasion by Germanic tribes seemed to sound the death knell for the Western Roman Empire. Historians have examined both the internal conditions that weakened the expansive empire and the external force of the barbarian invasions and have presented a variety of explanations for the fall of the Western Roman Empire.

◆ **Directions:** The following question is based on the accompanying documents in Part A. As you analyze the documents, take into account both the source of the document and the author's point of view. Be sure to:

1. Carefully read the document-based question. Consider what you already know about this topic. How would you answer the question if you had no documents to examine?

2. Now, read each document carefully, underlining key phrases and words that address the document-based question. You may also wish to use the margin to make brief notes. Answer the questions which follow each document.

3. Based on your own knowledge and on the information found in the documents, formulate a thesis that directly answers the question.

4. Organize supportive and relevant information into a brief outline.

5. Write a well-organized essay proving your thesis. The essay should be logically presented and should include information both from the documents and from your own knowledge outside of the documents.

Question: *What caused the fall of the Western Roman Empire?*

◆ **Part A:** The following documents address the causes for the fall of Rome. Examine each document carefully, and answer the questions that follow.

Document 1

This excerpt is from a textbook, *The Course of Civilization* by Strayer, Gatzke, and Harbison (Harcourt, Brace and World, Inc., 1961).

> The basic trouble was that very few inhabitants of the empire believed that the old civilization was worth saving . . . the overwhelming majority of the population had been systematically excluded from political responsibilities. They could not organize to protect themselves; they could not serve in the army. . . . Their economic plight was hopeless. Most of them were serfs bound to the soil, and the small urban groups saw their cities slipping into uninterrupted decline.

What were the basic problems facing the Western Roman Empire according to these authors?

_____

_____

(continued)

DBQ 2: Fall of the Western Roman Empire *(continued)*

Document 2

This is an excerpt from *The Decline and Fall of the Roman Empire* by Edward Gibbon.

> The decline of Rome was the natural and inevitable effect of immoderate greatness [large size] . . . The introduction . . . of Christianity, had some influence on the decline and fall of the Roman empire. The clergy successfully preached the doctrine of patience; the active virtues of society were discouraged; and the last remains of military spirit were buried in the cloister; a large portion of public and private wealth was consecrated to the . . . demands of charity and devotion. . . .

According to this excerpt from Gibbon, what were two causes for the fall of Rome? Explain both.

_____

_____

_____

_____

Document 3

This excerpt is from *Uses of the Past* by Herbert J. Muller.

> First the economic factor . . . While the empire was expanding, its prosperity was fed by plundered wealth and by new markets in the semi-barbaric provinces. When the empire ceased to expand, however, economic progress soon ceased. . . .
>
> The abundance of slaves led to the growth of the *latifundia*, the great estates that . . . came to dominate agriculture and ruin the free *coloni* [farmers] who drifted to the cities, to add to the unemployment there. The abundance of slaves likewise kept wages low.

What economic issues does Muller identify as causes for decline? Explain. _____

_____

_____

_____

How was slavery a cause for the decline of the Roman Empire? _____

_____

_____

(continued)

*Document-Based Assessment
Activities for Global History Classes*

DBQ 2: Fall of the Western Roman Empire *(continued)*

Document 4

This excerpt, from *The New Deal in Old Rome* by Henry Haskell, blames the decline on the heavy taxation required to support the government's expenses.

> . . . Part of the money went into . . . the maintenance of the army and of the vast bureau-cracy required by a centralized government . . . the expense led to strangling taxation. . . . The heart was taken out of enterprising men . . . tenants fled from their farms and business-men and workmen from their occupations. Private enterprise was crushed and the state was forced to take over many kinds of business to keep the machine running. People learned to expect something for nothing. The old Roman virtues of self-reliance and initiative were lost in that part of the population on relief [welfare]. . . . The central government under-took such far-reaching responsibility in affairs that the fiber of the citizens weakened.

Why did the Roman government have large expenses? _____

_____

What was the effect of high taxation on the people? _____

_____

What effect did the establishment of a governmental welfare system have on the people?

_____

_____

Document 5

This excerpt, from *Romans Without Laurels* by Indro Montanelli, blames the fall on "internal decay," specifically that of the military.

> Rome, like all great empires, was not overthrown by external enemies but undermined by internal decay. . . . The military crisis was the result of . . . proud old aristocracy's . . . short-age of children. [Consequently] foreigners poured into this . . . void [lack of soldiers]. The Roman army [was] composed entirely of Germans.

What does this author identify as the cause of problems in the military? _____

_____

_____

(continued)

DBQ 2: Fall of the Western Roman Empire (continued)

Document 6

This map shows the barbarian invasions of the Roman Empire prior to 476.

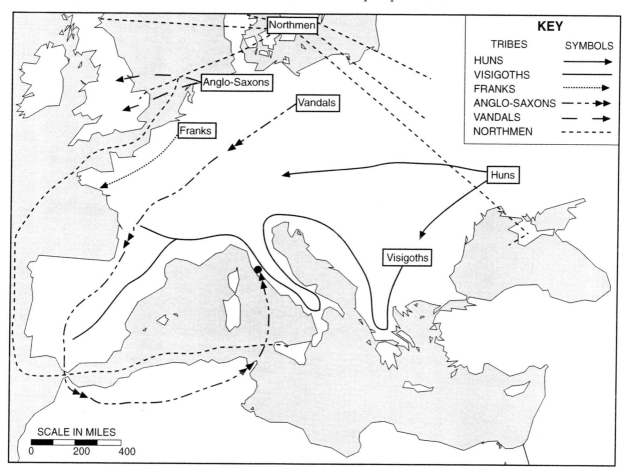

According to the map above, what was the cause of the fall of the Roman Empire? _____
_____
_____

Was this a unified attack? _____

◆ **Part B—Essay**

> *What caused the fall of the Western Roman Empire?*

Grading Key

Document 1

The Romans did not feel the empire was worth saving. They became apathetic. The majority were serfs and had been excluded from the government and from the army. Farming was declining as well as the cities.

Document 2

The Roman Empire fell because it was too large in size. They had conquered too much and were unable to keep control over the many parts. In addition, Christianity weakened the empire because it required its followers to be loyal to another more peaceful God.

Document 3

Several economic issues are addressed. When the empire stopped expanding, its markets and economic progress also stopped. Slavery took jobs away from the free peasants, and because they could not compete with slaves, became either tenant farmers or unemployed city dwellers.

Document 4

The government needed money for the army, the bureaucracy, and welfare. High taxation drove private owners out of business. The government was forced to take over. People on welfare lost their initiative, and this weakened the moral fiber of the empire.

Document 5

The problem in the military was due to the shortage of Roman soldiers and the inclusion of German barbarians in their places.

Document 6

The map shows the barbarian invasions from the East. It shows how the barbarians attacked the empire on all sides and took control of various parts of the empire.

Additional Information Beyond the Documents

The documents provide students with only fragments of evidence. Answers should include relevant information from beyond just the documents—information that students have learned from their classroom study. The following list suggests some of the concepts, people, and events that students could use in their essays from their outside learning.

The multiple causes and conditions in the Western Roman Empire—political, social, economic, and military—that led to the fall

The Germanic tribes

The gradual decline, rather than "fall," of the Roman Empire

Political:
Lack of orderly succession for emperors
Government corruption
Extensive empire difficult to rule/run

Social:
Lack of patriotism, morality
Luxury of wealthy
Class distinctions

Economic:
Small farmers lost their land, increases in welfare for unemployed
Heavy taxation
Slavery increases

Sample Student Essay and Suggested Grading

Although the Roman Empire was truly affected by external threats, I believe that it fell as a result of internal decay. Two influential internal causes of the fall were economy and social issues. Slavery, high taxes, and government spending contributed to economic decline. Also the attitudes of the people greatly affected the future of the already weakening Western Roman Empire.

First, the economy proved to be a factor in the decline of the empire. Slavery was the cause of a great increase in unemployment, as the use of slaves in the workforce took over the jobs of peasants and "ruined the free peasantry." *(Document 3)* Many people lost their businesses and jobs. *(Document 3)* Another economic situation involved the government and its high taxes, as well as spending. The central government of the Roman Empire was forced to increase taxes, as the price of keeping up the large empire increased. "There were land taxes, property taxes, occupation taxes, poll taxes." *(Document 4)* The high taxes were difficult to manage, and again, many were left poor. However, government spending was also a problem. Money the government earned from taxes went mainly to the "bureaucracy required by a central government," and the ". . . maintenance of the army." *(Document 4)* In addition, social situations also contributed to the fall of the Roman Empire.

Social issues, including the spread of Christianity as well as the feelings of the people toward the Roman Empire greatly influenced the decline. As Christianity spread throughout the empire, the outlook of people on life and the treatment of others changed. "Love thy neighbor" and salvation in order to reach heaven caused the people to become more thoughtful of others and less devoted to the emperor. This situation hurt the military, where "remains of military spirit were buried in the cloister." *(Document 2)* These men lost their fight, their war-like ways as this new religion taught the evilness and sin in hurting others. Thus, the military grew weak. Also, the people of the empire had a poor outlook concerning the future on earth. As a result of the internal decay that was obvious in the major cities of the empires, ". . . very few inhabitants of the empire believed that the old civilization was worth saving." *(Document 1)* When the people living in the empire could not find pride for their land, the empire began to weaken, as people either left or did not get involved in the central government's efforts to try to improve certain situations.

In conclusion, the combined economic and social conflict truly influenced the fall of the Western Roman Empire. I firmly believe that issues like slavery, taxes, and the spread of Christianity caused defeat for this once strong and powerful empire. It has been said that Rome wasn't built in a day; but also true was that it didn't fall in one day either. This process of decay and corruption occurred over a period of 100 years. But still, the strongest empire in the world fell, never to be repeated, again.

Teacher Comments

This essay addresses the required aspects of the topic—internal or external causes for the fall of the Western Roman Empire. It includes relevant outside details, facts, and examples. The writer incorporates the outside information and the documents into the body of a well organized essay, which includes an introduction and conclusion. Score: level 5. This is a good DBQ essay written early in the ninth grade as part of a unit test.

DBQ 3: The Middle Ages: Dark Ages, Age of Faith, Age of Feudalism, or a Golden Age?

Historical Context

The Middle Ages in Europe, a period of time from approximately A.D. 500 to 1400, have been referred to by a variety of terms—the Age of Faith, the Dark Ages, the Age of Feudalism, and even a Golden Age. The medieval era began with the destruction of the Roman Empire and the disorder that followed, which led to the rise of feudalism. During this period of darkness, the Roman Catholic Church provided spiritual direction as well as many nonreligious functions for the people of the times. Many literary, artistic, and architectural advances occurred.

◆ **Directions:** The following question is based on the accompanying documents in Part A. As you analyze the documents, take into account both the source of the document and the author's point of view. Be sure to:

1. Carefully read the document-based question. Consider what you already know about this topic. How would you answer the question if you had no documents to examine?

2. Now, read each document carefully, underlining key phrases and words that address the document-based question. You may also wish to use the margin to make brief notes. Answer the questions which follow each document.

3. Based on your own knowledge and on the information found in the documents, formulate a thesis that directly answers the question.

4. Organize supportive and relevant information into a brief outline.

5. Write a well-organized essay proving your thesis. The essay should be logically presented and should include information both from the documents and from your own knowledge outside of the documents.

Question: *Which labels for the Middle Ages best describe the era between 500 and 1400 in Europe: The Dark Ages, the Age of Feudalism, the Age of Faith, or the Golden Age of Europe? You must discuss three labels.*

◆ **Part A:** The following documents provide information about the Middle Ages in Europe. Examine each document carefully, and answer the questions that follow.

(continued)

DBQ 3: The Middle Ages (continued)

Document 1

In *The Middle Ages,* historian Frantz Funck-Brentano made use of previously published texts to describe Europe in the ninth and tenth centuries (Heinemann, 1922, pp. 1–3).

> The barbarians have broken through the ramparts. The Saracen [Moors] invasions have spread in successive waves over the South. The Hungarians swarm over the Eastern provinces . . . they sacked town and village, and laid waste the fields. They burned down the churches and then departed with a crowd of captives. . . . There is no longer any trade, only unceasing terror. . . . The peasant has abandoned his ravaged fields to avoid the violence of anarchy. The people have gone to cower in the depths of the forests or in inaccessible regions, or have taken refuge in the high mountains. . . . Society has no longer any government. . . .

According to the author, what were conditions like in Europe during the 800's?

_____

_____

Document 2

This excerpt is from the Homage Oath taken by John of Toul.

> I, John of Toul, make known that I am the liege man of the [count and countess of Champagne]. . . . I will aid the count of Champagne in my own person, and will send to the count and countess of Champagne the knights whose service I owe to them for the fief which I hold of them. . . ."

What are the obligations John is promising to uphold? _____

_____

Document 3

The Anglo-Saxon Chronicle tells of invasions of England.

> | 842 | In this year there was a great slaughter in London and Quentavic and in Rochester. |
> | 846 | According to their custom the Northmen plundered . . . and burned the town of Dordrecht. . . . the Northmen, with their boats filled with immense booty, including both men and goods, returned to their own country. . . . |

According to this Chronicle, what is happening at this time (842–846)? _____

_____

(continued)

DBQ 3: The Middle Ages (continued)

Document 4

FEUDAL OBLIGATIONS

Vassal to lord: Lord to vassal:

| *Obligation:* |
| Loyalty |
| Military service |
| Ransom, if needed |

→

←

| *Obligation:* |
| Protection |
| Land (fief) |

Explain the mutual obligations as illustrated in this diagram. _____

_____

_____

_____

_____

Document 5

A Church council calls for the observance of the Truce of God, 1083.

> . . . That from the first day of the Advent of our Lord through Epiphany . . . and throughout the year on every Sunday, Friday, and Saturday, and on the fast days of the four seasons . . . this decree of peace shall be observed . . . so that no one may commit murder, arson, robbery, or assault, no one may injure another with a sword, club, or any kind of weapon. . . . On . . . every day set aside, or to be set aside, for fasts or feasts, arms may be carried, but on this condition, that no injury shall be done in any way to any one . . . If it shall happen that any castle is besieged during the days which are included within the peace, the besiegers shall cease from attack unless they are set upon by the beseiged and compelled to beat the latter back. . . .

According to this document, what is the Church trying to accomplish? _____

_____

_____

_____

_____

(continued)

DBQ 3: The Middle Ages (continued)

Document 6

This excerpt describes the Middle Ages. (From Gray C. Boyce, "The Medieval Period" in *The 34th Yearbook of the National Council for the Social Studies*, 1964, pp. 69–70.)

> . . . we learn that an age once traditionally described as "dark" had remarkable vitality and exuberance. Even at its worst it performed the function of guarding, frequently by accident and chance, the knowledge and treasures of what had come before, but even more it was creative and inventive, and transmitted to later ages great riches of its own.

What functions were provided during the Middle Ages according to this author?

_____

_____

_____

_____

_____

Document 7

This description of the positive aspects of the Middle Ages was taken from *Medieval Europe* by H. C. Davis, Oxford University Press, 1946, p. 79.

> . . . Medieval culture was imperfect, was restricted to a narrow circle of superior minds. . . . Measure it, however, by the memories and the achievements that it has bequeathed to the modern world, and it will be found not unworthy to rank with those of earlier and later Golden Ages. It flourished in the midst of rude surroundings, fierce passions, and material ambitions . . . we must judge of them by their philosophy and law, by their poetry and architecture. . . .

How does this author describe the era? _____

_____

_____

_____

_____

(continued)

DBQ 3: The Middle Ages (continued)

Document 8

This excerpt is from the monastic vows of Brother Gerald.

> I hereby renounce my parents, my brothers and relatives, my friends, my possessions . . . and the vain and empty glory and pleasure of this world. I also renounce my own will, for the will of God. I accept all the hardships of the monastic life, and take the vows of purity, chastity, and poverty, in the hope of heaven; and I promise to remain a monk in this monastery all the days of my life.

What is Gerald promising to do when he becomes a monk? _____

_____

_____

_____

Document 9

In 1095, Pope Urban II issued a call for a holy crusade—a war to recapture the Holy Land.

> . . . Your brethren who live in the [Middle] East are in urgent need of your help. . . . For, as most of you have heard, the Turks and the Arabs have attacked them and have conquered the territory of Romania [the Byzantine Empire]. . . . They have occupied more and more of the lands of those Christians. . . . They have killed and captured many, and have destroyed the churches and devastated the Empire. . . . All who die by the way, whether by land or sea, or in battle against the pagans, shall have immediate remission of sins.

How does this call for a crusade demonstrate the power of the Pope and the Catholic Church?

_____

_____

_____

_____

(continued)

DBQ 3: The Middle Ages *(continued)*

Document 10

Examine this picture of a Gothic cathedral. How does it illustrate the power of the Catholic Church?

_____

_____

_____

_____

◆ **Part B—Essay**

Which labels for the Middle Ages best describe the era between 500 and 1400 in Europe: The Dark Ages, the Age of Feudalism, the Age of Faith, or the Golden Age of Europe? You must discuss three labels.

Document-Based Assessment
Activities for Global History Classes

Grading Key

Document 1

Anarchy dominated in Europe due to the barbarian attacks—the Moors in the South and the Hungarians in the East. Towns, villages, and churches were destroyed; there was no more trade; peasants were leaving their fields. It was the Dark Ages.

Document 2

In this fuedal oath John of Toul is promising his service and that of his knights.

Document 3

According to the Anglo-Saxon Chronicle, the Northmen were plundering and burning cities and taking captives back to their country. The Saracens, or Moors, were slaughtering Christians and taking prisoners.

Document 4

These are feudal obligations. The vassal promises his loyalty, military service, and ransom payment to his lord. In return, the lord promises his vassal that he will provide a fief and protection.

Document 5

In the Truce of God, the Catholic Church was trying to limit fighting on specific days. This is evidence of the power of the Church.

Document 6

This writer points out that during the Middle Ages the knowledge of the past was protected. Even more, the Middle Ages were "creative and inventive"—a Golden Age of sorts.

Document 7

This author believed that medieval culture ranked with that of earlier Golden Ages due to its philosophy, law, poetry, and architecture. Its greatest achievement, however, was the belief that service to others and to God is most important.

Document 8

A monk promises to give up pleasures and possessions of this world. He takes vows of poverty, chastity, and purity, and promises to do service to God for his lifetime.

Document 9

In the Pope's call for a crusade, he was asking western Europeans to go to the aid of their fellow Christians in the Byzantine Empire who were under a fierce attack by the Arabs and Turks. The Pope demonstrated his power by stating that anyone who died on the crusade would have his sins forgiven.

Document 10

The spires of the Gothic cathedral point to heaven, the ultimate goal of the medieval man or woman. The cathedral was built to honor God. Its beautiful stained-glass windows, arches, flying buttresses, and sculpture illustrate the power of the Catholic Church.

Additional Information Beyond the Documents

The documents provide students with only fragments of evidence. Answers should include relevant information beyond the documents—information that students have learned from their classroom study. The following list suggests some of the information that students might include in the essay.

Dark Ages—invasions, fall of Western Roman Empire
Feudalism, manoral system, vassals, fiefs, nobles, serfs
The many political, social, religious, and economic roles and power of the Catholic Church—
     sacraments, clergy, nuns, excommunication, teaching, tithing
The art, architecture, and literary accomplishments of late Middle Ages, Gothic cathedrals, crusades
Pope Urban II, vernacular

Sample Student Essay and Suggested Grading

The Middle Ages, a period of time from the year A.D. 50 through 1400 have been referred to by a variety of terms including the Age of Faith, Feudalism, the Dark Ages, and a Golden Age. However, the three terms I believe describe this the most completely are the Age of Faith, Feudalism, and Golden Age.

Faith was an important aspect in medieval life. The Catholic Church was very powerful, for the clergy had influence on government as well as religion. Men of the church made laws of behavior for the people and helped the God-fearing Christians perform the sacraments, which ensured a place in heaven. The main goal for medieval citizens was to go to heaven, and the church controlled that decision of who was to go and who was not. If a certain person was found to be disobeying the rules of the church, they were excommunicated, and were shunned from the church, therefore ruining their chance to go to heaven. Even the king himself feared the power of God and the Pope. In addition many men and women became monks and nuns, proclaiming that they would ". . . renounce their own will for the will of God," and ". . . take the vows of purity, chastity, and poverty." (Document 8) The monks and nuns provided health care, and relgious education to the common people, therefore influencing medieval life.

The medieval period was also a feudal age. Social classes were rigid and strict, and one couldn't marry between them. The nobles were the upper class, the peasants and serfs the lower. Medieval lords would receive fiefs or pieces of land from a higher lord or the king himself. Eventually, this lord would distribute the land among other lower lords, called vassals. In return for the land the vassals owed loyalty and military service. The lord promised protection from invaders to the vassal in addition to the land. Vassals usually had peasants or serfs working the land, and knights that provided military strength. Lords also had knights for protection. As stated in Document 2, vassals remained very loyal to their Lords; "I will aid the Count of Champagne . . . and will send knights whose service I owe to them for the fief which I hold of them." The manors that the feudalistic system originated were self-sufficient, for everything that was needed for survival was on this piece of land. A church for religion, fields to grow food, a mill for grinding, water from the well, and housing for the serfs in addition to the large manorhouse for the lord were all stationed in this one large area called the manor.

(continued on next page)

Sample Student Essay and Suggested Grading

(*continued*)

Lastly the Middle Ages were a Golden Age. In the later Middle Ages, there was a need for education and learning; the government needed more literate men for bureacracies, and the clergy requested a better education. Cathedrals which served as evidence of this Golden Age developed into the very first universities. In these schools, Europeans studied works of Aristotle, theology, and philosophy. Roman numerals were soon replaced by the easier to use Arabic number system. Medieval students also studied medicine and math, especially in the area of geometry. This ". . . age once described as 'dark' had . . . vitality and exuberance . . . they were creative and inventive." (Document 6) Literature written in the "vernacular" language, or common languages of French and Italian, started to be popular during the Middle Ages. A few examples are the *Divine Comedy* and *The Canterbury Tales.* Lastly, the building of the beautiful Gothic cathedrals with the high ceilings, stained-glass windows and flying buttresses were an example of the architectural feats of this time. As stated in document 7, "It flourished in the midst of rude surroundings . . . we must judge them of their philosophy and law, poetry and architecture. (They) sprung from the soil and ripened in the atmosphere of a civilized society."

In conclusion, the Middle Ages was a time of many occurrences, but most certainly it was a time of faith, feudalism, and the thirst for knowledge.

Teacher Comments

This student essay thoroughly addresses all aspects of the task. It identifies three labels that best describe the Middle Ages. It includes information from most of the documents as well as much relevant outside information, facts, and details. It weaves the documents in the body paragraphs and includes an introduction and conclusion. It is a well-organized, well-developed essay. Score: level 5.

DBQ 4: Middle Ages or Early Renaissance?
Differing Interpretations

Historical Context:

According to the humanist writers and thinkers of the fifteenth and sixteenth centuries, the Middle Ages were a thousand years of ignorance and superstition. These Renaissance men who saw themselves as leaders in an era of rebirth and learning looked to the ancient Greeks and Romans for models in literature and art as their view of man and his world. Some historians questioned this interpretation, with its sharp division between the Middle Ages and the Renaissance. Instead they pointed out evidence of increased intellectual activity starting in the medieval universities. The debate centers around whether the Renaissance was a unique age or a continuation of the Middle Ages.

◆ **Directions:** The following question is based on the accompanying documents in Part A. As you analyze the documents, take into account both the source of the document and the author's point of view. Be sure to:

1. Carefully read the document-based question. Consider what you already know about this topic. How would you answer the question if you had no documents to examine?

2. Now, read each document carefully, underlining key phrases and words that address the document-based question. You may also wish to use the margin to make brief notes. Answer the questions which follow each document.

3. Based on your own knowledge and on the information found in the documents, formulate a thesis that directly answers the question.

4. Organize supportive and relevant information into a brief outline.

5. Write a well-organized essay proving your thesis. The essay should be logically presented and should include information both from the documents and from your own knowledge outside of the documents.

> **Question:** *Was the Renaissance, with its unique advances, a period distinct from the Middle Ages or was it a continuation—the high point—of the Middle Ages?*

◆ **Part A:** Examine each document carefully, and answer the questions that follow.

Document 1

This excerpt is from The *Renaissance* by Wassace K. Ferguson (New York: Holt, 1940, pp. 1–3).

> The idea that there was a great revival or rebirth of literature and the arts, after a thousand years of cultural sterility, in the fourteenth and fifteenth centuries originated with the Italian writers of the Renaissance themselves. Finding the feudal and ecclesiastical literature and Gothic art of the Middle Ages uncongenial to their taste, they turned for inspiration to the civilization of Roman and Greek antiquity. . . . Thus, from the beginning, the double conception of medieval darkness and subsequent cultural rebirth was colored by the acceptance of classical standards.

(continued)

DBQ 4: Middle Ages or Early Renaissance? Differing Interpretations (*continued*)

According to Ferguson, how did writers and thinkers of the fifteenth and sixteenth centuries view themselves? Were they part of the Middle Ages or a different era—the Renaissance?

_____

Document 2

This excerpt is from *The Civilization of the Renaissance in Italy,* (1878) by Jacob Burchhardt.

> In the Middle Ages both sides of human consciousness lay dreaming or half awake beneath a common veil. The veil was woven of faith, illusion, and childish prepossession. . . . Man was conscious of himself only as member of a race, people, party, family, or corporation— only through some general category. In Italy this veil first melted into air . . .; man became a spiritual individual, and recognized himself as such. In the same way the Greek had once distinguished himself from barbarian. . . .
>
> When this impulse to the highest individual development was combined with a powerful and varied nature, . . . then arose the "all-sided man". . . . in Italy at the time of the Renaissance we find artists who in every branch created new and perfect works, and who also made the greatest impression as men.

According to historian Jacob Burchhardt, was there a difference between the people of the Middle Ages and people of the Renaissance? Explain.

_____

_____

Document 3

This excerpt is from *A History of Europe from 1378 to 1494* written by W. T. Waugh.

> It has become evident that there was no suspension of intellectual life in medieval Europe. If there was a Revival of Learning, it occurred about the year A.D. 1000, since when human knowledge has never ceased to advance. It cannot even be said that the Humanists of the fourteenth and fifteenth centuries revived the study of the classics. Scholars had been nourished on the classics for centuries. . . . In the first place, the classical writer most studied in the Middle Ages was a Greek, Aristotle. . . . And actually the medieval scholars of western Europe were acquainted with most of the Latin authors familiar to us. . . .
>
> The merits of the artists and the influence of the Humanist scholars must be acknowledged. But one must beware of exaggerating the practical results of their work. It is undeniable that very few people knew or cared anything about the sayings or doings of the Humanists. . . . [and] the plain fact remains that the masterpieces of Renaissance sculpture can have been seen by few, those of Renaissance painting by fewer. And in those days, unless you actually saw them, you could not tell what they were like. . . .

(*continued*)

DBQ 4: Middle Ages or Early Renaissance?
Differing Interpretations (continued)

According to historian W. T. Waugh, when did modern culture and the work of the humanists begin? Was there a renaissance? What evidence does he cite for his point of view?

_____

_____

_____

Document 4

The following is an excerpt from *Petrarch's Secret,* translated by W. H. Draper, 1911.

> My principle is that, as concerning the glory from which we may hope for here below [on earth], it is right for us to seek it while we are here below. One may expect to enjoy that other more radiant glory in heaven, when we shall have there arrived, and when one will have no more care or wish for the glory of earth. Therefore, as I think, it is in the true order that mortal men should first care for mortal things. . . .

According to Petrarch, a humanist, with what should man be concerned? Is this similar or different from the interests of medieval man? Explain.

_____

_____

_____

Document 5

This excerpt is from *Life and Letters of Erasmus* by A. J. Froude, 1894.

> The world is waking out of a long deep sleep. The old ignorance is still defended. Time was when learning was only found in the religious orders. The religious orders nowadays care only for money and sensuality [indulgence of the appetites], while learning has passed to secular princes and peers and courtiers. Where in school or monastery will you find so many distinguished and accomplished men as form your English Court? Shame on us all! The tables of priests and divines run with wine and echo with drunken noise and scurrilous jest, while in princes' halls is heard only grave and modest conversation on points of morals or knowledge. . . . That king of yours [Henry VIII of England] may bring back the golden age, though I shall not live to enjoy it, as my tale draws to an end.

According to Erasmus, what change is coming? How does he feel about priests, the church, and the religious order? Why do you think he feels this way? _____

_____

_____

(continued)

DBQ 4: Middle Ages or Early Renaissance? Differing Interpretations *(continued)*

Document 6

These sketches were done by Leonardo daVinci.

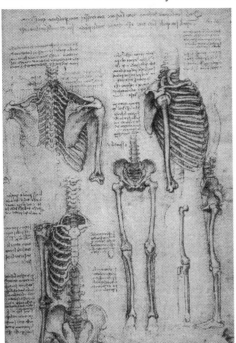 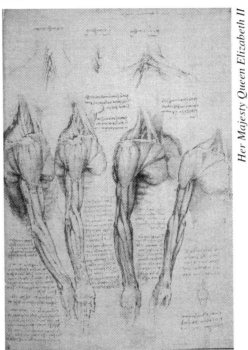

Her Majesty Queen Elizabeth II

What do these drawings tell you about the interests and abilities of daVinci? Explain.

_____

_____

_____

_____

Document 7

Johannes Kepler, a German astronomer, made this observation in 1596.

> Now we shall proceed to the astronomical determination of the orbits and to geometrical considerations. If these do not confirm the thesis, then all our previous effects have doubtless been in vain.

According to Kepler, how are theories proven? Is this consistent with the attitude of a "medieval" scientist? Explain. _____

_____

_____

_____

(continued)

*Document-Based Assessment
Activities for Global History Classes*

DBQ 4: Middle Ages or Early Renaissance? Differing Interpretations (continued)

Document 8
Universities founded in the twelfth through fifteenth centuries

12th–13th Century	14th Century	15th Century
ITALY		
Salerno Bologna Vicenza, 1204 Arezzo, 1215 Padua, 1222 Naples, 1224 Vercelli, 1228 Siena, 1246 Curia Romana, 1244–1245	Rome (Studium Urbis), 1303 Perugia, 1308 Pisa, 1343 Florence, 1349 Pavia, 1361 Ferrara, 1391	Turin, 1405 Catania, 1444
FRANCE		
Paris Orleans, *ante* 1231 Angers Toulouse, 1229, 1233	Avignon, 1303 Cahors, 1332 Grenoble, 1339 Orange, 1365	Aix, 1409 Dôle, 1422 Poitiers, 1431 Caen, 1432 Bordeaux, 1441 Valence, 1452, 1459 Nantes, 1460 Bourges, 1464 Besançon, 1485
GREAT BRITAIN		
Oxford Cambridge, 1209		S. Andrews, 1415 Glasgow, 1451 Aberdeen, 1494
SPAIN AND PORTUGAL		
Valladolid, c. 1250 Palencia, 1212–1214 Salamanca, *ante* 1230 Seville, 1254, in 1260 (Latin and Arabic) Lisbon-Coimbra, 1290	Lerida, 1300 Perpignan, 1349 Huesca, 1359	Barcelona, 1450 Saragossa, 1474 Palma (Majorca), 1483 Siguenza, 1489 Alcalá, 1499 Valencia, 1500
GERMANY, BOHEMIA, AND THE LOW COUNTRIES		
	Prague, 1347–8 Vienna, 1365 Erfurt, 1379, 1392 Heidelberg, 1385 Cologne, 1388	Würzburg Leipzig, 1409 Rostock, 1419 Louvain, 1425 Trier, 1454, 1473 Griefswald, 1428, 1456 Freiburg-im-Breisgau, 1455–1456 Basel, 1459 Ingolstadt, 1459, 1472 Mainz, 1476 Tübingen, 1476–1477

(continued)

DBQ 4: Middle Ages or Early Renaissance? Differing Interpretations *(continued)*

What does the chart tell you about the times and places where universities were founded? What conclusion can you draw about learning during the Middle Ages?

_____

_____

_____

_____

_____

_____

_____

◆ **Part B—Essay**

> *Was the Renaissance, with its unique advances, a period distinct from the Middle Ages or was it a continuation—the high point—of the Middle Ages?*

Grading Key

Document 1

Writers and thinkers of the fifteenth and sixteenth centuries introduced the idea that they were a part of a distinct era—the Renaissance. They looked at ancient Greek and Roman civilizations for models. They found the ideals of the ancient Greeks and Romans to be superior to those found in the feudal and religious literature of the Middle Ages.

Document 2

Burchhardt identified a difference between the medieval man, who was controlled by faith throughout his life, and the Renaissance man, who strove for the highest individual development. The medieval man is not an individual, but rather one in a group. The Renaissance man wanted to be unique, to stand out, to be different and to make an impression on others. This man was aware of the real world and was talented in many fields.

Document 3

In contrast, W. T. Waugh found little evidence of a distinct period. Rather, he saw continual intellectual activity throughout medieval Europe. If there was a renaissance, it began in 1000, during the Middle Ages, not with the humanists of the fourteenth and fifteenth centuries. Medieval scholars read the Greek and Roman classics. Therefore the humanists have exaggerated their importance. The "renaissance" was no more than the high point of the Middle Ages.

Document 4

Petrarch was a humanist who was concerned with things of this world—not heaven. He was a man of the Renaissance.

Document 5

Erasmus was critical both of the religious orders and the Church, who, he believed, were interested only in money and drink. In contrast, Erasmus viewed the secular rulers as knowledgeable leaders. He admired the English court and King Henry VIII, who, he hoped, would provide leadership.

Document 6

DaVinci, a complex man of the Renaissance, was interested in anatomy and the realistic portrayal of the human body. He was the ideal man of the Renaissance due to his many talents and interests.

Document 7

Kepler, an astronomer, used observation and mathematics to prove his thesis. He did not accept what he was told by the Church or the ancients. Instead, he proved his theories.

Document 8

The chart shows the many universities founded in the twelfth through fifteenth centuries, leading to the conclusion that there were centers of learning established and thriving in Italy, France, and Great Britain throughout the Middle Ages.

Additional Information Beyond the Documents

The documents provide students with only fragments of evidence. Answers should include relevant information beyond just the documents—information that students have learned from their classroom study. The following list suggests some of the concepts, people, and events that students could use in their essays from their outside learning.

Medieval art, science, literature, attitude toward life	Renaissance individuals, art, science, literature, and attitude toward life

DBQ 5: Byzantine Empire under Justinian

Historical Context:

When Justinian became emperor in 527, he was determined to revive the ancient Roman Empire, to build a new Rome. He established Constantinople as the capital of the Byzantine or Eastern Roman Empire and preserved Roman heritage for more than a thousand years.

◆ **Directions:** The following question is based on the accompanying documents in Part A. As you analyze the documents, take into account both the source of the document and the author's point of view. Be sure to:

1. Carefully read the document-based question. Consider what you already know about this topic. How would you answer the question if you had no documents to examine?

2. Now, read each document carefully, underlining key phrases and words that address the document-based question. You may also wish to use the margin to make brief notes. Answer the questions which follow each document.

3. Based on your own knowledge and on the information found in the documents, formulate a thesis that directly answers the question.

4. Organize supportive and relevant information into a brief outline.

5. Write a well-organized essay proving your thesis. The essay should be logically presented and should include information both from the documents and from your own knowledge outside of the documents.

> **Question:** *Evaluate the reign of Emperor Justinian. Did he revive the Roman Empire in the Byzantine Empire? What is his legacy?*

◆ **Part A:** The following documents deal with the reign of Justinian and the Byzantine Empire. Examine each document carefully, and answer the questions that follow.

Document 1

This description of Justinian is from *Buildings* by Procopius, Justinian's official court historian.

> Justinian created countless cities which did not exist before. And finding that the belief in God was . . . straying into errors . . . he brought it about that it stood on the firm foundation of a single faith. Moreover, finding the laws obscure because they had become far more numerous than they should be, and in obvious confusion because they disagreed with each other. He preserved them [in the Legal Code of Emperor Justinian, A.D. 529] . . . by controlling their discrepancies with the greatest firmness.

According to Procopius, what are three contributions of Justinian?

_____

_____

_____

(continued)

DBQ 5: Byzantine Empire under Justinian (continued)

Document 2

Justinian was described by Procopius in a different book, the *Secret History,* which was published after his death.

> Justinian was . . . crafty, hypocritical, secretive by temperament, two-faced: a clever fellow with marvelous ability to conceal his real opinion . . . lying all the time. . . .

Which characteristics of Justinian does Procopius stress in the *Secret History?* _____
_____

Why is this description so different from Document 1? _____
_____

Document 3

Justinian ruled like earlier Roman emperors. This is a description of him by a Byzantine official.

> The emperor is equal to all men in the nature of his body, but in the authority of his rank he is similar to God, who rules all.

How is Justinian's power explained? _____
_____

Document 4

This excerpt, also written by Procopius, describes the Hagia Sophia upon its completion in 537.

> In height it rises to the very heavens. . . . A spherical-shaped dome . . . makes it exceedingly beautiful: from the lightness of the building it does not appear to rest upon a solid founda-tion, but to . . . be suspended from heaven by the fabled golden chain. . . . The entire ceiling is covered with pure gold, which adds glory to the beauty, though the rays of light reflected upon the gold from the marble surpass it in beauty. . . . And whenever anyone enters this church to pray, he understands at once that it is not by any human strength or skill, but by the influence of God, that this work has been perfected. And so his mind is lifted up toward God. . . . Moreover, it is impossible to describe the treasure of gold and silver plate and gems, which the Emperor Justinian has presented to it. . . .

What are the distinctive characteristics of the Hagia Sophia? _____
_____

What impact does the church have on a visitor? _____
_____

(continued)

Name_____ Date_____

DBQ 5: Byzantine Empire under Justinian (continued)

Document 5

Justinian was a great builder. This is evident from the fortifications and buildings he constructed in Constantinople, shown on the map below.

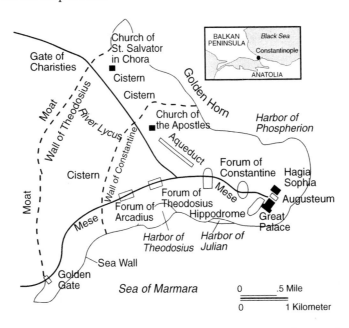

Study this map of Constantinople and describe the building projects that made it the center of power. In addition, discuss Constantinople's strategic location for trade and defense.

_____

_____

_____

_____

_____

_____

_____

(continued)

DBQ 5: Byzantine Empire under Justinian *(continued)*

Document 6

The Byzantine Empire reached its greatest size under Justinian. From 565 until its collapse in 1453, several invaders took sections of the empire.

The Byzantine Empire in 527

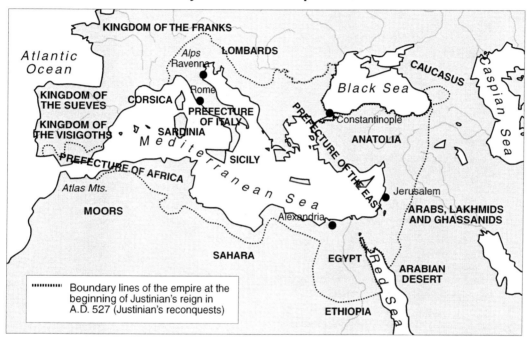

Describe the areas that were included in the Byzantine Empire. _____

_____

_____

_____

_____

_____

◆ **Part B—Essay**

Evaluate the reign of Justinian. Did he revive the Roman Empire in the Byzantine Empire? What is his legacy?

Grading Key

Document 1

Justinian built cities; he restored the Byzantine Empire to one faith, and he organized a uniform legal code.

Document 2

At the same time Procopius saw Justinian as a liar and a hypocrite. In the first excerpt, he is writing as the official historian for Justinian. The *Secret History* is his personal, and perhaps more honest, description.

Document 3

Justinian ruled with absolute power, as he was "similar to God."

Document 4

The Hagia Sophia is noteworthy because of its height. It "rises to the heavens" and is rectangular in shape, with arches on all sides as well as a dome on top. Inside the "light reflects upon the gold" of the ceiling. There is a feeling of light and beauty throughout the huge church. Consequently, a visitor feels that this is a work built with the "influence of God" and thus raises one's attention to God.

Document 5

This map shows Constantinople's location on the Sea of Marmara, part of the waterway system that connects the Black Sea to the Aegean Sea. Its location made Constantinople a center of trade for goods coming from Asia, Africa, and Europe. As for defense, Constantinople was surrounded on three sides by water, which protected it from attack. It also had a moat, the Wall of Theodosius, and the Wall of Constantine as fortifications on its west side. In addition to the walls that were built for protection, Justinian rebuilt Hagia Sophia, enlarged the palace, built roads, aqueducts, and provided entertainment in the Hippodrome. All of these projects demonstrated the power of the emperor and of the Byzantine Empire.

Document 6

The Byzantine Empire, with Constantinople as its capital, included Asia Minor, the Balkans, Greece, Italy, Egypt, and the coasts of North Africa and southern Spain. The cost of regaining part of the empire from the Germanic tribes and protecting it from attacks from the east left the treasury depleted.

Additional Information Beyond the Documents

The documents provide students with only fragments of evidence. Answers should include relevant information beyond just the documents—information that students have learned from their classroom study. The following list suggests some of the information that students might include in their essays from their outside learning.

Extent of Roman Empire and its legacy—law, engineering, literature, history

Justinian's Code

fortification of Constantinople

Hagia Sophia

Preserved Greek and Roman works—philosophy, literature, math, history, as well as contributions mentioned in the documents

Name_____   Date_____

DBQ 6: Spread of Islamic Civilization

Historical Context:

From its beginnings in Arabia to its extensive empire encompassing the Middle East, parts of Asia, North Africa, and parts of Europe, the spread of Islam in the late 600's and 700's has drawn much study. The spread of Islamic beliefs and civilization have been described from a variety of perspectives.

◆ **Directions:** The following question is based on the accompanying documents in Part A. As you analyze the documents, take into account both the source of the document and the author's point of view. Be sure to:

1. Carefully read the document-based question. Consider what you already know about this topic. How would you answer the question if you had no documents to examine?

2. Now, read each document carefully, underlining key phrases and words that address the document-based question. You may also wish to use the margin to make brief notes. Answer the questions which follow each document.

3. Based on your own knowledge and on the information found in the documents, formulate a thesis that directly answers the question.

4. Organize supportive and relevant information into a brief outline.

5. Write a well-organized essay proving your thesis. The essay should be logically presented and should include information both from the documents and from your own knowledge outside of the documents.

> **Question:** *How did Islamic civilization spread to encompass such an extensive empire? What practices or methods were used to spread Islam?*

◆ **Part A:** The following documents will help you understand the methods used to spread Islam. Examine each document carefully, and answer the questions that follow.

Document 1

In this excerpt, Mohammed gives choices to the leader of a Christian Arab tribe.

> Believe or else pay tribute [money] . . . obey the Lord and His Apostle [Mohammed], and he will defend you. . . . But if ye oppose and displease them . . . I will fight against you and take captive your little ones and slay the elder. . . .

What alternatives does Mohammed offer to the leader of the Christian Arab tribe?

_____

_____

_____

_____

(continued)

DBQ 6: Spread of Islamic Civilization (continued)

Document 2

This quotation from the Quran offers specific directions.

> Ye shall do battle with them, or they shall profess Islam . . . whosoever shall obey God and His Apostle, He shall bring him into the gardens of [Paradise]; but whosoever shall turn back, He will punish him. . . .

What does Mohammed offer to Muslims who follow him? _____
_____
_____

Document 3

This excerpt from *History of the Arabs*, by Philip K. Hitti, explains the Muslim view on equality. (London: Macmillan & Co. Ltd., 1946.)

> We have witnessed a people [Muslims] to each and every one of whom death is preferable to life, and humility to prominence, and to none of whom this world has the least attraction. Their leader is like one of them: the low cannot be distinguished from the high, nor the master from the slave. And when the prayer time comes, all wash their hands and feet and humbly pray.

How does this writer describe the Muslim people? _____
_____
_____

Document 4

This description of the Battle of Tours in 732, from *Fifteen Decisive Battles of the World* by Sir Edward Crecy (E. P. Dutton & Co., Inc.), provides a perspective on the Muslim fighting style.

> The Moslems struck their enemies and laid waste to the country and took captives without number . . . everything gave way to their scimitars [swords]. . . . All the nations of the Franks trembled as that terrible army . . . attacked Tours . . . and the fury and cruelty of the Moslems towards the inhabitants of the city were like the fury and cruelty of raging tigers.

How does this writer describe the methods and conquests of the Muslim army at the Battle of Tours?
_____
_____
_____

(continued)

DBQ 6: Spread of Islamic Civilization (continued)

Document 5

This excerpt suggests that there are options to conversion depending on the religion of the people facing conversion. (From J. J. Saunders, "The Caliph Omar: Arab Imperialist," in *History Today*, March, 1961, pp. 180–181.)

> Koranic revelation commanded them to "Fight in the cause of God against those who fight you, but do not be the aggressors." The early Muslims thus fought their heathen enemies. . . . war against unbelievers was sanctioned by divine revelation and the example of the Prophet.
>
> But many Arabs were Jews or Christians: What was to be done with them? Mohammed respected the older monotheistic faiths . . . he called them "People of the Book" . . . they were not forced into Islam but were allowed to retain their ancestral religion on payment of tribute.

According to this writer, why was conversion required? _____

_____

How were Jews and Christians to be treated? _____

_____

Document 6

In this excerpt from *The Spirit of Islam*, by a Muslim writer, Syed Ameer Ali (London: Chatto and Windus, 1964), the expansion of Islam is defended and that of Christianity criticized.

> Islam never interfered with the dogmas of any moral faith, never persecuted . . . Islam "grasped the sword" in self defense; Christianity grasped it in order to stifle freedom of thought and liberty of belief. Wherever Christianity prevailed, no other religion could be followed without molestation. The Moslems, on the other hand, required from others a simple guarantee of peace, tribute in return for protection, of perfect equality—on condition of the acceptance of Islam. . . .

How does this Muslim writer view the expansion of Islam? _____

_____

_____

What specific words make you aware of his contrasting view of Christianity? _____

_____

How and why does his viewpoint differ from that expressed in Document 5? _____

_____

_____

(continued)

35   *Document-Based Assessment*
                                                                Activities for Global History Classes

DBQ 6: Spread of Islamic Civilization *(continued)*

Document 7

Philip K. Hitti, in *History of the Arabs* (MacMillan, 1946), offers another explanation for conquest.

> The passion to go to heaven in the next life may have been operative with some, but the desire for the comforts and luxuries of the civilized regions of the Fertile Crescent was just as strong in the case of many. . . . The campaigns seem to have started as raids to provide new outlets for the warring tribes, the objective in most cases being booty [riches] and not the gaining of a permanent foothold. . . . The movement acquired momentum as the warriors passed from victory to victory . . . the creation of the Arab empire followed inevitably.

According to this writer, how is the expansion of Islam explained? _____
_____

How does his explanation differ from those expressed in Documents 5 and 6? _____
_____

Document 8

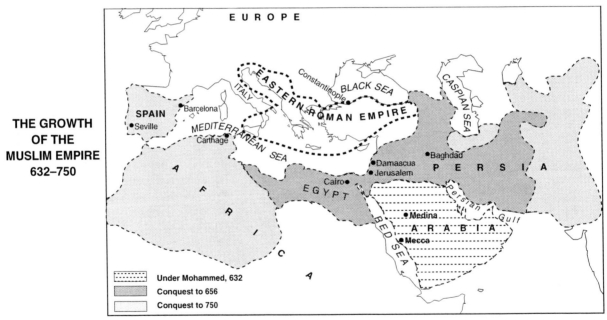

THE GROWTH OF THE MUSLIM EMPIRE 632–750

Under Mohammed, 632
Conquest to 656
Conquest to 750

This map shows the growth of Islam between 632 and 750. Describe what the map reveals about the extensive area included in the Muslim Empire by 750. _____
_____

◆ **Part B—Essay**

> *How did Islamic civilization spread to encompass such an extensive empire?*
> *What practices or methods were used to spread Islam?*

Document-Based Assessment
Activities for Global History Classes

Grading Key

Document 1

The Christian Arab tribe could either convert to Islam or pay a tribute. If they converted, the Lord would protect them. If not, they would face a fight.

Document 2

The Quran offers "Paradise" to those who follow Mohammed.

Document 3

According to Hitti, the Muslims were not interested in this world and its rewards. Rather, they were a group of prayerful people who treated all equally.

Document 4

The Muslims cruelly destroyed their enemies as well as the land and cities under attack.

Document 5

The early Muslims fought "their heathen enemies" because war against them was required by the Quran and the example of the Prophet. But Jews and Christians, since they were "People of the Book," or Bible, were not forced to convert to Islam. They could pay a tribute and remain true to their faiths.

Document 6

This Muslim views the expansion of Islam as an act of self-defense rather than of aggression. They are a peace-loving people who provide protection and equality in return for acceptance of Islam. In contrast, he says Christians have "grasped the sword in order to stifle freedom of thought." The Islamic writer is empathetic to the Muslim point of view because it is his religion.

Document 7

According to Hitti, for most Muslims it was the desire for the riches of the people of the Fertile Crescent and something for the warring tribes to do that acted as motivation for expansion. He seems to have been less interested in religious factors and more interested in military and economic issues.

Document 8

The map shows that the Islamic Empire spread from the Arabian peninsula, across North Africa to Spain.

Additional Information Beyond the Documents

The documents provide students with only fragments of evidence. Answers should include relevant information from beyond the documents—information that students have learned from their classroom study. The following list suggests some of that information.

| Beliefs and practices of Islam | The map of Africa, Asia, and Europe | The ways of spreading a religion: conquest, conversion, cultural interaction |

DBQ 7: Islamic Civilization: Its Contributions to World Culture

Historical Context:

The Muslims inherited much from Greece, Rome, and India and adopted much from the people they conquered. Because of their tolerance of other cultures, they were able to advance scholarship in several areas to the highest level at that time. As a result, Muslim achievements stand out and have a lasting impact on world cultures.

◆ **Directions:** The following question is based on the accompanying documents in Part A. As you analyze the documents, take into account both the source of the document and the author's point of view. Be sure to:

1. Carefully read the document-based question. Consider what you already know about this topic. How would you answer the question if you had no documents to examine?

2. Now, read each document carefully, underlining key phrases and words that address the document-based question. You may also wish to use the margin to make brief notes. Answer the questions which follow each document.

3. Based on your own knowledge and on the information found in the documents, formulate a thesis that directly answers the question.

4. Organize supportive and relevant information into a brief outline.

5. Write a well-organized essay proving your thesis. The essay should be logically presented and should include information both from the documents and from your own knowledge outside of the documents.

> **Question:** *What were the most important Islamic achievements? Why were the Muslims able to make such great contributions and how did these contributions impact the world?*

◆ **Part A:** The following documents will help you understand Islamic achievements. Examine each document carefully, and answer the questions that follow.

Document 1

This excerpt, from the textbook *World History: Patterns of Interaction* (Beck, Black, Naylor, Shabaka. Evanston, IL: McDougal Littell, 1999), explains why Muslims both preserved existing knowledge and extended it.

> Muslims had practical reasons for supporting the advancement of science. Rulers wanted qualified physicians treating their ills. The faithful . . . relied on mathematicians and astronomers to calculate the times of prayer and the direction of Mecca. . . . Their attitude reflected a deep-seated curiosity about the world and a quest for truth that reached back to . . . Mohammed himself. After the fall of Rome in A.D. 476, Europe entered a period of upheaval and chaos, an era in which scholarship suffered. . . . In the early 800's . . . the House of Wisdom opened in Baghdad. There, scholars of different cultures and beliefs worked . . . translating texts from Greece, India, Persia, and elsewhere into Arabic.

(continued)

DBQ 7: Islamic Civilization:
Its Contributions to World Culture (continued)

What were the reasons for Muslim interest in learning? _____
_____

Document 2

The Islamic capital of Cordova was described by a contemporary as the "jewel of the world." The Islamic schools and universities were preferred by European scholars such as Abelard and Roger Bacon. Philip Hitti describes Cordova in *Capital Cities of Arab Islam* (University of Minnesota Press, 1973).

> Besides the university library, Arab statisticians assure us the city boasted 37 libraries, numberless bookstores, 800 public schools . . . and a total population of 300,000. Its people enjoyed a high standard of living and refinement and walked on paved streets . . .—all this at a time when hardly a town in Europe, Constantinople excepted, counted more than a few thousand inhabitants. Parisians and Londoners were still trudging on muddy, dark alleys. . . .

What conditions in Cordova does this author cite as evidence of the high level of Islamic civilization and scholarship? _____
_____

Document 3

Physician al-Razi wrote a medical reference encyclopedia, the *Comprehensive Book and Treatise on Smallpox and Measles*. Ibn Sina (Avicenna) wrote the five-volume *The Canon of Medicine*. These books were translated into Latin and other languages and influenced doctors in Europe. The illustration below, from an Islamic medical book, and the explanation from the textbook *World History: Patterns of Interaction*, show the level of medical expertise of Islamic doctors.

> **Medical Reference Books**
>
> When Europeans learned that Muslims had preserved important medical texts, they wanted to translate the texts into Latin. In the eleventh century, scholars traveled to libraries in places such as Toledo, Spain, where they began translating—but only after they learned to read Arabic.
>
> Through this process, European medical schools gained access to vital reference sources such as al-Razi's *Comprehensive Book* and Ibn Sina's *The Canon of Medicine*. Ibn Sina's five-volume encyclopedia guided doctors of Europe and Southwest Asia for six centuries. For nearly 500 years, al Qasim's work, *The Method*, which contained original drawings of some 200 medical tools, was the foremost textbook on surgery in Europe.

What does this document tell you about Muslim medical knowledge? _____
_____

How did it impact Western civilization? _____
_____

(continued)

DBQ 7: Islamic Civilization: Its Contributions to World Culture *(continued)*

Document 4

Al-Khwarizmi, a Muslim mathematician, studied Indian sources and wrote a textbook in the 800's about *al-jabr* (the Arabic word for algebra), which was later translated into Latin and used throughout Europe. Muslim mathematicians also adopted Arabic numerals from the Indians and used them in a place-value system.

$$3x = 15$$

$$\begin{array}{r} 135 \\ + 20 \\ \hline 155 \end{array}$$

What is the importance of these mathematical advances? _____

_____

How did these developments impact Western civilization? _____

_____

Document 5

Using scientific observation and their understanding of mathematics and optics, Muslim scholars made advancements in trigonometry and astronomy as well as mapmaking. They used the astrolabe (Figure A) and the armillary sphere (Figure B) to study the skies and make calculations for their calendars and maps.

Figure A

Figure B

How did each of these instruments impact Muslim and Western civilization? _____

_____

_____

(continued)

DBQ 7: Islamic Civilization: Its Contributions to World Culture *(continued)*

Document 6

Muslim artists used calligraphy to decorate buildings and objects of art as well as to reflect the glory of Allah. Study this example and answer the questions that follow.

Why was calligraphy used in religious art?

_____

_____

_____

What impact has calligraphy had on world art?

_____

_____

_____

Document 7

Muslim architects blended features from various sources, including the Byzantine Empire, as well as added new features. Study this photo of the Dome of the Rock in Jerusalem, and answer the questions that follow.

What are the distinctive architectural features of this building? _____

_____

What impact did these architectural designs have on buildings throughout the world? _____

_____

(continued)

DBQ 7: Islamic Civilization:
Its Contributions to World Culture (continued)

Document 8

The standard for Arabic literature and poetry is the Quran, which influenced Sufi poets. Read these two excerpts and answer the questions that follow.

> In the name of the Merciful and Compassionate God. That is the Book! There is no doubt therein. . . . God, there is no God but He! He will surely assemble you on the resurrection day. . . .
>
> *Quran*
>
> As salt resolved in the ocean
> I was swallowed in God's sea. . . .
> Jalal al-Din Rumi—*Persian Poems*

Why is the Quran the model for poetry? _____

_____

_____

How did the Quran influence literature and poetry? _____

_____

_____

Document 9

Between 750 and 1350, the Muslim merchants built a trade network throughout their empire, as this excerpt from *The Gates of India* by Sir T. H. Holdich (London: MacMillan, 1910) explains.

> Masters of the sea, even as of the land, the Arabs spread throughout the geographical area. The whole world was theirs to explore . . . their ships sailed across the seas even as they moved across the land [Sahara Desert into West Africa]. The might of the sword of Islam carved the way for the slaveowner and the merchant to follow.

Why and where were the Muslims able to establish a trading empire? _____

_____

_____

_____

(continued)

DBQ 7: Islamic Civilization:
Its Contributions to World Culture *(continued)*

Document 10

Historian J. H. Kramers describes the benefits that Europeans received from Muslim industry in *The Legacy of Islam.* (Clarendon Press, Oxford, 1931)

First should be mentioned the textile products imported from Islamic countries: muslin . . . damask . . . gauze, cotton, satin.

Natural products, which by their name indicate they were imported from Islamic countries—fruits, like orange, lemon, and apricot; vegetables, like spinach, artichokes, and saffron. . . . Finally our commercial vocabulary itself has preserved . . . proofs that there was a time when Islamic trade and trade customs exercised a deep influence on the commercial development of Christian countries—such words as "traffic" [derived from Arabic *tafriq*], which means distribution.

What were the commercial or trade benefits that Europeans gained from Islamic commerce and

industry? _____

_____

_____

_____

◆ **Part B—Essay**

What were the most important Islamic achievements? Why were the Muslims able to make such great contributions and how did these contributions impact the world?

Grading Key

Document 1

As Muslims, they needed to know the direction of Mecca and the times for daily prayer. They were curious about this world in much the same way Mohammed was. The Muslim Empire became a center of learning because, after the fall of Rome, there was chaos in Europe. At the same time, Muslim rulers encouraged scholars to translate books into Arabic.

Document 2

Cordova, an Islamic city in Spain, was a center of learning for its inhabitants. They enjoyed the necessities of life and even some of the comforts that allowed for time to pursue learning in many fields.

Document 3

Muslims knew about diseases and medical procedures. They were more advanced than the Europeans.

Document 4

Muslims brought the number system of India back to Europe. It was easier to use than Roman numerals. Their work in algebra was translated and used throughout Europe.

Document 5

The astrolabe was used to measure the angles of the sun and stars. By lining up the top rings of the armillary sphere, astronomers could calculate the time of day or year. This information was used in mapmaking and on calendars.

Document 6

Calligraphy was used to glorify Allah. Since the Quran forbade the depicting of living beings, Muslims used calligraphy in decorative arts in their mosques, and on glass, ceramic, woodwork, and books.

Document 7

The gold dome and arches are important features of this mosque. There are also mosaic art and calligraphy, features that are seen in mosques around the world.

Document 8

The Quran is sacred to Muslims. It contains praise of God and Islam. The influence of God can be seen in the poem.

Document 9

Muslims traded on land and sea. They controlled land along the Mediterranean Sea and were able to cross the Sahara Desert with their camel caravans. As they spread their religion and conquered and expanded their empire, they created a trading network.

Document 10

As a result of trading with the Islamic merchants, Europeans acquired textiles, fruits, vegetables, and even new vocabulary.

Additional Information Beyond the Documents

The documents provide students with only fragments of evidence. Answers should include relevant information from beyond the documents—information that students have learned from their classroom study. The following list suggests some of that information.

Islamic beliefs and practices—Quran	Islamic achievements in medicine, math, science, calligraphy, literature, architecture—mosques	The civilizations included in the Islamic Empire, for example, India, North Africa, and trade

Name_____ Date_____

DBQ 8: Africa Before European Arrival

Historical Context:

Africans had developed advanced civilizations before the Europeans arrived in the fifteenth and sixteenth centuries. Beginning with Aksum (Ethiopia today) in East Africa in the 300's, kingdoms, empires, and cities arose and declined. In West Africa, three empires—Ghana, Mali, and Songhai—controlled the gold and salt trade. Between 1000 and 1500, cities on Africa's east coast also gained wealth and power through trade. There were several centers of advanced civilization in Africa between 300 and 1400.

◆ **Directions:** The following question is based on the accompanying documents in Part A. As you analyze the documents, take into account both the source of the document and the author's point of view. Be sure to:

1. Carefully read the document-based question. Consider what you already know about this topic. How would you answer the question if you had no documents to examine?

2. Now, read each document carefully, underlining key phrases and words that address the document-based question. You may also wish to use the margin to make brief notes. Answer the questions which follow each document.

3. Based on your own knowledge and on the information found in the documents, formulate a thesis that directly answers the question.

4. Organize supportive and relevant information into a brief outline.

5. Write a well-organized essay proving your thesis. The essay should be logically presented and should include information both from the documents and from your own knowledge outside of the documents.

> **Question:** *Evaluate the achievements of the African empires, kingdoms, and cities before the arrival of the Europeans.*

◆ **Part A:** Examine each document carefully, and answer the questions that follow.

Document 1

Aksum reached its height between 325 and 360. Aksum's location made it an important international trading center. This map shows the trade routes to and from Aksum between 300 and 700.

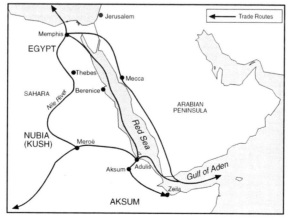

(continued)

Document-Based Assessment
Activities for Global History Classes

DBQ 8: Africa Before European Arrival (continued)

How did Aksum's location enable it to become a trading center? _____
_____

Document 2

Between 700 and 1067, the Kingdom of ancient Ghana rose in power and gained control of the trans-Saharan gold and salt trade. This description of the king's court in ancient Ghana was written by the Arab scholar, Al-Bakri in 1067. (*Through African Eyes,* ed. by Leon E. Clark, Praeger Press, Inc., New York, 1970.)

> The court of appeal is held in a domed pavilion around which stand ten horses with gold embroidered trappings. Behind the king stand ten pages holding shields and swords decorated with gold, and on his right are the sons of the subordinate kings of his country, all wearing splendid garments and with their hair mixed with gold. The governor of the city sits on the ground before the king, and around him are ministers seated likewise. At the door of the pavilion are dogs . . . [wearing] collars of gold and silver, studded with a number of balls of the same metals.

What evidence of wealth is described? _____
_____

What evidence of an advanced political structure is described? _____
_____

Document 3

This explanation for the wealth of the kingdom of Ghana is taken from *Through African Eyes,* ed. by Leon E. Clark, Praeger Press, New York, 1970.

> The Arab traders of this region wanted gold as much as the Wangara wanted salt, but both had to pass through Ghana to trade. . . . Ghana controlled the land . . . it had the military forces . . . to maintain peace in the area, thereby assuring safe trade for the Arabs and the Wangara.
>
> Ancient Ghana was an extremely complex empire. It possessed many of the characteristics of powerful nations today: wealth based on trade, sufficient food to feed its people, income derived from taxes, social organization that ensured justice and efficient political control, a strong army equipped with advanced weapons, and a foreign policy that led to peace and cooperation with other people.

Explain ancient Ghana's role in the gold-salt trade. _____
_____
_____

(continued)

DBQ 8: Africa Before European Arrival (continued)

What characteristics of an advanced civilization did ancient Ghana possess? _____

_____

_____

Document 4

Mansa Musa expanded the Mali empire to twice the size of the Ghana empire it replaced. On his *haj* to Mecca, Mansa Musa stopped in Cairo, Egypt, and was described by an Egyptian official in this way:

> This man Mansa Musa, spread upon Cairo the flood of his generosity: there was no person, officer of the court, or holder of any office of the Sultanate who did not receive a sum of gold from him.

What about Mansa Musa impressed the Egyptian official? _____

_____

Document 5

In this excerpt, a Moroccan traveler, using the name Leo Africanus, describes the city of Timbuktu.

> Here are many doctors, judges, priests, and other learned men that are well maintained at the king's costs. Various manuscripts and written books are brought here . . . and sold for more money than other merchandise.

What about Timbuktu impressed this writer? _____

_____

Document 6

Ibn Battuta traveled in Mali in 1352 and wrote this description in *Travels to Kingdom of Mali*.

> They are seldom unjust, and have a greater abhorrence [hatred] of injustice than any other people. Their sultan shows no mercy to anyone who is guilty of the least act of it. There is complete security in their country. Neither traveler nor inhabitant in it has anything to fear from robbers.

What two things impressed Ibn Battuta about Mali? _____

_____

_____

(continued)

DBQ 8: Africa Before European Arrival (continued)

Document 7

This description of the lost-wax process of making bronze sculpture comes from an oral account of a Hausa artisan.

> In the name of Allah the Compassionate, the Merciful. This account will show how the [Benin] figures are made. This work is one to cause wonder. Now this kind of work is done with clay, and wax, and red metal [copper], and solder [zinc] and lead, and fire. . . . Next it is set aside to cool, then [the outside covering of clay] is broken off. Then you see a beautiful figure. . . .

Why is this bronze statue described as a "wonder"? _____

_____

Document 8

Ibn Battuta also visited Kilwa, an East African coastal city-state, in 1331 and described it as one of the most beautiful cities in the world. He admired the luxury enjoyed by the Muslim rulers and merchants. Kilwa controlled the overseas trade between the interior of Africa and sites around that part of the world. Study this map of East African trade in A.D. 1000, and answer the questions below.

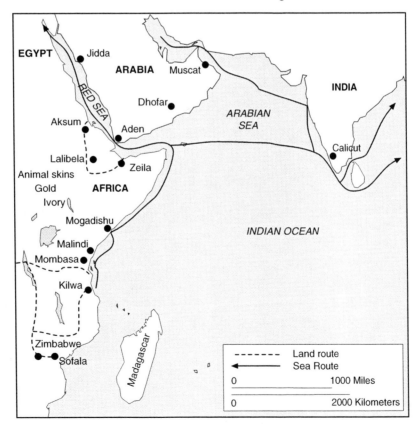

(continued)

*Document-Based Assessment
Activities for Global History Classes*

DBQ 8: Africa Before European Arrival (continued)

The sea routes connected what areas (countries and cities)? _____

_____

_____

_____

_____

What products were brought from the interior of Africa to Kilwa by the land route? _____

_____

_____

_____

_____

◆ **Part B—Essay**

> *Evaluate the achievements of the African empires, kingdoms, and cities before the arrival of the Europeans.*

Grading Key

Document 1

Aksum's location on the Red Sea provided it with extensive coastline and ports and access to the countries on both the Mediterranean Sea and Indian Ocean. Therefore, Aksum traded with India, Greek and Roman cities, and areas in the Far East. The caravan routes connect Aksum to Egypt and to the interior of Africa.

Document 2

The wealth of Ghana is evident in the gold in the horses' equipment, the shields of the pages, and the collars of the dogs. The advanced political system is evident in the organization the king assembled—the governor and ministers.

Document 3

Since Ghana has no gold or salt, it controls the land and "maintains peace" so that "trade is safe." The characteristics of an advanced civilization possessed by Ghana include food, money to provide a strong, well-equipped army, and an efficient government.

Document 4

He was impressed with the amount of gold that Mansa Musa had and with his willingness to give it away.

Document 5

He saw Timbuktu as a center of "learned men" who were supported by the king. Books were highly valued there.

Document 6

Ibn Battuta was impressed with the justice and security enjoyed by all the people of Mali.

Document 7

The bronze statue was produced using molten metals and wax displacement process. The statue is very detailed.

Document 8

The sea routes connect Kilwa to the Red Sea, the Indian Ocean, and the Arabian Sea. As a result, Kilwa connected sites in the Arabian peninsula, India, and the Far East with those in Africa and Europe. The products brought from the interior of Africa included gold, ivory, and animal skins.

Additional Information Beyond the Documents

The documents provide students with only fragments of evidence. Answers should include relevant information from beyond the documents—information that students have learned from their classroom study. The following list suggests some of that information.

Trade patterns and products in West Africa, East Africa
Art and architecture of each kingdom and empire—Aksum, Ghana, Mali, Songhai
Governmental organization
Learning, language, and belief systems
Cultural diffusion and blending

DBQ 9: Civilizations of the Americas

Historical Context:

Between 300 and 1500, three advanced civilizations developed in Central and South America. Ruins from the Mayan civilization remain even today in southern Mexico, Guatemala, and Honduras. The Aztecs, who conquered most of Mexico, built a highly-developed civilization in the 1400's. At the same time, the Incas were building an empire in Peru.

◆ **Directions:** The following question is based on the accompanying documents in Part A. As you analyze the documents, take into account both the source of the document and the author's point of view. Be sure to:

1. Carefully read the document-based question. Consider what you already know about this topic. How would you answer the question if you had no documents to examine?

2. Now, read each document carefully, underlining key phrases and words that address the document-based question. You may also wish to use the margin to make brief notes. Answer the questions which follow each document.

3. Based on your own knowledge and on the information found in the documents, formulate a thesis that directly answers the question.

4. Organize supportive and relevant information into a brief outline.

5. Write a well-organized essay proving your thesis. The essay should be logically presented and should include information both from the documents and from your own knowledge outside of the documents.

Question: *How advanced were the Mayan, Aztec, and Incan civilizations? What were their major accomplishments?*

◆ **Part A:** Examine each document carefully and answer the questions that follow.

Document 1

This Mayan pyramid temple in Tikal was the tallest structure in the Americas until the twentieth century.

(continued)

DBQ 9: Civilizations of the Americas *(continued)*

Describe the significance of Mayan architecture evidenced in this temple at Tikal. _____

_____

Document 2

This is a glyph from the Mayan calendar.

What is the significance of this glyph (symbol)? _____

_____

Document 3

When he arrived in 1519, the Spanish conqueror Hernán Cortés described the magnificent Aztec capital of Tenochtitlán with these words.

> The city has many squares where markets are held and trading is carried on. There is one square . . . where there are daily more than 60,000 souls, buying and selling, and where are found all the kinds of merchandise produced in these countries, including food products, jewels of gold and silver, lead, brass, copper, zinc, bones, shells, and feathers.

Why was Cortés impressed when he arrived in Tenochtitlán in 1519? _____

_____

Document 4

This description of farming in the Incan empire in 1539 was provided by Garciasco de la Vega, a son of an Incan princess and a Spanish explorer.

> As soon as the Incan ruler had conquered any kingdom and set up his government, he ordered that the farmland used to grow corn be extended. For this purpose, he ordered irrigation channels to be constructed. The engineers showed great cleverness and skill in supplying water for the crops, since only scattered sections of the land could grow corn. For this reason, they endeavored to increase its fertility as much as possible.

What engineering technique was described by this sixteenth-century author? _____

_____

Why was this a significant achievement? _____

_____

(continued)

DBQ 9: Civilizations of the Americas *(continued)*

Document 5

This map shows the Incan Empire in 1565.

How did the Incan government unite its empire in the Andes Mountains?

_____

_____

_____

What is the significance of this accomplishment?

_____

_____

_____

_____

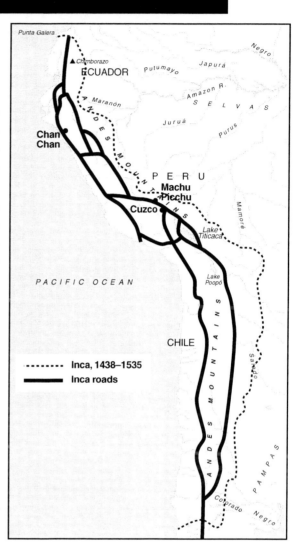

Document 6

This photo of the ruins of Machu Picchu provides evidence of the superior building design and farming techniques of the Inca in Peru.

What specific farming and building techniques were used by the Incas? _____

_____

_____

◆ **Part B—Essay**

How advanced were the Mayan, Aztec, and Incan civilizations? What were their major accomplishments?

*Document-Based Assessment
Activities for Global History Classes*

Grading Key

Document 1

This pyramid temple is evidence of the architectural skills of the Mayans. They were able to build monumental temples of stone, which they dedicated to both the gods and important rulers.

Document 2

This hieroglyphic symbol, or glyph, is part of the advanced writing system of the ancient Mayans. The Mayans used this writing system to record important historical events in stone.

Document 3

Tenochtitlán was the capital of the Aztec Empire. It was a bustling city, a market center where foods and "all kinds of merchandise" were bought and sold. This impressed Cortés when he arrived in 1519.

Document 4

The need to feed the people of the extensive Incan empire led engineers to develop an irrigation system so that corn and other crops could be grown on land that otherwise might not have been productive.

Document 5

The map shows the roads and trails that the Inca constructed to unite the people throughout the empire. Great engineering skills were involved in building roads, bridges, tunnels, and steps to cross rivers and mountains. The Inca built one of the greatest road systems in the world.

Document 6

The ruins of Machu Picchu, the Incan city built by the Incas in the Andes Mountains, remain today as evidence of the great building skills of the Incas. They fitted stones together without mortar and built houses that have survived earthquakes for centuries. They terraced mountainsides to increase the farmland available to grow crops.

Additional Information Beyond the Documents

The documents provide students with only fragments of evidence. Answers should include relevant information from beyond the documents—information that students have learned from their classroom study. The following list suggests some of the information that students might include in their essays from their outside learning.

Mayans:
Mexico
Central America
Palenque
city-state
religion—many gods
writing system
math, astronomy, calendars
farming and trading

Incas:
Peru
sun-god king
religion—many gods
government—centralized
united—common language
engineers—roads, bridges

Aztecs:
Mesoamerica
pyramid builders
city builders
religion—many gods
government—king
pictorial written language
trade

DBQ 10: Causes of the French Revolution

Historical Context:

The French Revolution of 1789 had many long-range causes. Political, social, and economic conditions in France contributed to the discontent felt by many French people—especially those of the third estate. The ideas of the intellectuals of the Enlightenment brought new views of government and society. The American Revolution also influenced the coming of the French Revolution.

◆ **Directions:** The following question is based on the accompanying documents in Part A. As you analyze the documents, take into account both the source of the document and the author's point of view. Be sure to:

1. Carefully read the document-based question. Consider what you already know about this topic. How would you answer the question if you had no documents to examine?
2. Now, read each document carefully, underlining key phrases and words that address the document-based question. You may also wish to use the margin to make brief notes. Answer the questions which follow each document.
3. Based on your own knowledge and on the information found in the documents, formulate a thesis that directly answers the question.
4. Organize supportive and relevant information into a brief outline.
5. Write a well-organized essay proving your thesis. The essay should be logically presented and should include information both from the documents and from your own knowledge outside of the documents.

> **Question:** *What were the most important causes of the French Revolution? (Discuss three.)*

◆ **Part A:** Examine each document carefully, and answer the questions that follow.

Document 1

This excerpt is adapted from *Travels in France* by Arthur Young, who traveled through France from 1787 to 1789.

> In the south of France there is a taille [tax on the land and its produce]. There is an injustice in levying the amount each person must pay. Lands held by the nobility are taxed very little. Lands held by commoners are taxed heavily. . . .
>
> September 5, 1788: The poor people seem very poor indeed. The children are terribly ragged.
>
> June 10, 1789: The lack of bread is terrible. Stories arrive every moment from the provinces of riots. . . . The price of bread has risen above people's ability to pay. This causes great misery.
>
> July 1789: . . . I was joined by a poor woman who complained of the hard times. "The tailles and feudal dues [rents owed the lords] are crushing us," she said.

List three observations this traveler made about the life of the peasant in France between 1787 and 1789. _____

(continued)

DBQ 10: Causes of the French Revolution *(continued)*

Document 2

This diagram illustrates the three estates in 1789 and the land each held during the Old Regime.

FIRST ESTATE	SECOND ESTATE	THIRD ESTATE
Clergy	Nobles	Middle class, peasants, city workers
1% of the people owned 10% of the land	2% of the people owned 35% of the land	97% of the people owned 55% of the land

What conclusions can you draw about the relationship between the percentage of the population in each estate and the percentage of land owned by that estate? _____

_____

What unfair conditions existed in pre-revolutionary France? _____

_____

Document 3

These are excerpts from the *cahiers* (lists of grievances about the king, taxing, and voting in the Estates General) brought to the Estates General.

That the king be forced to reform the abuses and tyranny of lettre de cachet.

That every tax . . . be granted [by the Estates General] only for a limited time.

That the taille [a tax on land] be borne equally by all classes. . . .

The meetings of the Estates General . . . shall be scheduled for definite times. . . .

in order to assure the third estate the influence it deserves because of its numbers . . . its votes in the assembly should be taken by head. . . .

What three changes did the third estate demand be made in the French government? _____

_____

_____

_____

(continued)

DBQ 10: Causes of the French Revolution (continued)

Document 4

In *The French Revolution,* historian Albert Mathiez claims that leadership fell to the middle class with their knowledge of the ideas of the Enlightenment.

> The Revolution had been accomplished in the minds of men long before it was translated into fact. . . .
>
> The middle class . . . was sensitive to their inferior legal position. The Revolution came from them—the middle class. The working classes were incapable of starting or controlling the Revolution. They were just beginning to learn to read.

What was the result of the middle class's knowledge of the ideas of the Enlightenment?

_____

_____

_____

Document 5

Lord Acton suggested another point of view.

> The condition of France alone did not bring about the overthrow of the monarchy . . . for the suffering of the people was not greater than they had been before. The ideas of the philosophs were not directly responsible for the outbreak . . . [but] the spark that changed thought into action was supplied by the Declaration of American Independence. . . . The American example caused the Revolution to break out. . . .

What did Lord Acton believe caused the French Revolution? _____

_____

_____

◆ Part B—Essay

> *What were the most important causes of the French Revolution? (Discuss three.)*

Grading Key

Document 1

Young described the lives of the peasants and their hardships—the hard work they had to do, the taxes they paid, the shortage of bread, and the high prices that they could not afford to pay. He highlights the inequity of the poorest class of citizens being forced to pay heavy taxes while the wealthiest citizens were taxed very little.

Document 2

The diagram shows how very few people occupied the first and second estates, yet how they held a large percentage of the land. The third estate, which included the most people, held less than 50 percent of the land.

Document 3

The *cahiers* contains the changes that the third estate want made in the French government. Specifically, they want an end to the *lettre de cachet;* they want the Estates General to meet regularly, and they want taxes to be levied by the Estates General.

Document 4

This author believed that the ideas of the Enlightenment had been in the minds of the people for a long time before action was taken. He adds that the middle class led the revolution because of their education.

Document 5

Lord Acton believed that the American Revolution and the Declaration of Independence spread revolutionary ideas to France and helped to bring the revolution.

Additional Information Beyond the Documents

The documents provide students with only fragments of evidence. Answers should include relevant information from beyond the documents—information that students have learned from their classroom study. The following list suggests some of the information that students might include in their essays from their outside learning.

The ideas of Enlightenment writers—Locke, Rousseau, Voltaire
Abuses of the Old Regime—incompetent absolute monarch Louis XVI
Economic problems—extravagant life at Versailles for the king and nobility
       aid to the American Revolution
       poor grain harvests
Rigid class system and the opposition of the bourgeoisie
Bankruptcy of the French government
Calls for reform

Sample Student Essay and Suggested Grading

The French Revolution, which commenced in 1789, had a long list of causes. The most important long-range causes of this revolution, however, were the ideas of the Enlightenment, the unfair taxes, the gap between the rich and poor, and the American Revolution and Declaration of Independence.

The ideas of the Enlightenment influenced the French Revolution. The third estate, or the poorest social group, held very little rights socially or politically. But some of them, like doctors and lawyers, were educated and could read the new ideas of government from philosophers such as John Locke, Montesquieu, and Rousseau. "The revolution had been accomplished in the minds of men long before it was translated into fact . . ." *(Document 4)* These men spoke of democratic governments, with certain freedoms and natural rights. Eventually, the people of the third estate began to question their own government in France, and by the standards of these philosophers, demanded change. The cahiers *(Document 3)* reflect the ideas of the Enlightenment—democracy and equality.

As an economic cause, the unfair taxes also proved a cause for the French Revolution. Again, the third estate, composed of merchants, doctors, lawyers, and peasants, were taxed very heavily on many things; "In the south of France there is a taille (a tax on the land and its produce) . . ." *(Document 1)* "Lands held by commoners are taxed heavily." Peasants also paid taxes to the clergy, nobles, and government. However, the richest estates, the clergy and nobles, paid little taxes or none at all despite their excess money, large land plots, and position and interaction with the government. "Lands held by the nobility were taxed very little." *(Document 1)* This unfair system angered the third estate, and prompted revolution.

As a social cause, in France there was a large gap between the rich and poor. A diagram *(Document 2)* shows this gap—there are very few members in the first and second estates, yet they owned the most land, while the third estate made up most of the population, yet owned very little land. In addition, as a political cause, the third estate had no privileges or say in the government, while both the clergy and nobles did. And as mentioned before, the inequality of taxes proved another gap in the social classes. These "rules caused the formation of just upper and lower classes, no real middle. The third-estate population didn't have any way to move up in the social pyramid as a result of these restrictions. The middle class (of the third estate) was sensitive to their inferior legal position. Revolution came from them." *(Document 4)*

Finally, the influence of the American Revolution and the Declaration of Independence helped spur the French Revolution. Lord Acton *(Document 5)* stated, ". . . the spark that changed thought into action was supplied by the Declaration of American Independence. . . . The American example caused the Revolution. . . ." By the colonists' influence, the French learned that if a small group of people could take on and defeat England, a very powerful country, they could do the same. The Americans helped encourage the Frenchmen's desire for freedom and democracy.

In conclusion, the French Revolution had its beginnings in many areas, but mostly in the inequalities felt by the common people, the new ideas of democracy and personal rights, and the examples of other revolutionists around them.

Teacher Comments

This essay addresses all aspects of the task—identifies three major causes of the French Revolution. It includes outside information, details, and examples. It incorporates references to most of the documents. The essay is well organized and has a strong introduction and conclusion. Score: level 5.

Name _____ Date _____

DBQ 11: Absolutism and Democracy

Historical Context:

Various forms of political systems have been used throughout world history. As nation-states were built in Europe, absolute monarchs with vast power and wealth ruled countries such as France and Russia. At the same time in England attempts were made to limit royal power and to protect the rights of some of the people. There was tension between absolutism and democracy. In studies of absolutism and democracy advantages and disadvantages for each governmental system can be identified. What form of government was most effective for this period of history?

◆ **Directions:** The following question is based on the accompanying documents in Part A. As you analyze the documents, take into account both the source of the document and the author's point of view. Be sure to:

1. Carefully read the document-based question. Consider what you already know about this topic. How would you answer the question if you had no documents to examine?

2. Now, read each document carefully, underlining key phrases and words that address the document-based question. You may also wish to use the margin to make brief notes. Answer the questions which follow each document.

3. Based on your own knowledge and on the information found in the documents, formulate a thesis that directly answers the question.

4. Organize supportive and relevant information into a brief outline.

5. Write a well-organized essay proving your thesis. The essay should be logically presented and should include information both from the documents and from your own knowledge outside of the documents.

> **Question:** *What form of government was most effective—democracy or absolutism—for the seventeenth and eighteenth centuries?*

◆ **Part A:** The following documents relate to different types of government. Examine each document carefully, and answer the questions that follow.

Document 1

This is an excerpt from *The Prince,* written by Machiavelli (fifteenth century).

> For all men in general this observation may be made: they are ungrateful, fickle, and deceitful, eager to avoid dangers, and avid for gain, and while you are useful to them they are all with you, but when it [danger] approaches they turn on you. Any prince, trusting only in their works and having no other preparations made, will fall to ruin, for friendships that are bought at a price and not by greatness and nobility of soul are paid for indeed, but they are not owned and cannot be called upon in time of need. Men have less hesitation in offending a man who is loved than one who is feared, for love is held by a bond of obligation which, as men are wicked, is broken whenever personal advantage suggests it, but fear is accompanied by the dread of punishment, which never relaxes.

What type of ruler must the prince be, and why is it necessary for him to rule in this manner?

_____

DBQ 11: Absolutism and Democracy (continued)

Document 2

These ideas were expressed by King James I of England in 1609.

> The state of monarchy is the supremest thing upon earth; for kings are not only God's lieu-tenants upon earth, and sit upon God's throne, but even by God Himself they are called gods. . . . Kings are justly called gods, for that they exercise a . . . divine power upon earth. . . . God hath power to create or destroy, make or unmake at His pleasure, to give life or sent death, to judge all and to be judged nor accountable to none, to raise low things and to make high things low at His pleasure . . . And the like power have kings . . .

What type of government does King James describe, and why does he believe it should be organized in this way? _____
_____
_____

Document 3

These ideas were expressed by King Louis XIV of France in 1660.

> The head alone has the right to deliberate and decide, and the functions of all the other members consist only in carrying out the commands given to them. . . . The more you grant . . . [to the assembled people], the more it claims . . . The interest of the state must come first.

What type of government does King Louis describe and why does he recommend this type of government? _____
_____
_____

Document 4

The following is an excerpt from Voltaire's writings.

> . . . I may disapprove of what you say, but I will defend to the death your right to say it. . . . The best government seems to be that in which all ranks of men are equally protected by the laws. . . .

What type of government does Voltaire recommend? What specific freedom does he feel is essential?
_____
_____
_____
_____

(continued)

DBQ 11: Absolutism and Democracy (continued)

Document 5

This excerpt is from John Locke's *Two Treatises on Government,* written in 1690.

> Men being . . . by nature all free, equal, and independent, no one can be . . . subjected to the political power of another without his own consent. . . . To protect natural rights governments are established. . . . Since men hope to preserve their property by establishing a government, they will not want that government to destroy their objectives. When legislators try to destroy or take away the property of the people, or try to reduce them to slavery, they put themselves in to a state of war with the people who can then refuse to obey the laws.

Why is government established? What type of government is described by Locke? Under what circumstances can the people revolt? _____

_____

_____

_____

_____

Document 6

The following is an excerpt from *The Spirit of the Laws,* written by Montesquieu in 1748.

> Although the forms of state—monarchy, aristocracy, and democracy—were united in English government, the powers of government were separated from one another. There can be no liberty where the executive, legislative, and judicial powers are united in one person or body of persons, because such concentration is bound to result in arbitrary despotism.

What type of government does Montesquieu describe and why does he believe it should be organized in this way? _____

_____

_____

_____

_____

◆ **Part B—Essay**

> *What form of government was most effective—democracy or absolutism—for the seventeenth and eighteenth centuries?*

Grading Key

Document 1

Because men are untrustworthy and "wicked," the ruler must instill fear in his subjects. They must fear him rather than love him if he wants to maintain control.

Document 2

King James I believed in "divine right." Consequently, he felt that the king is God's lieutenant and sits in His place on earth. Kings have "like power" to God. They have the power to do anything they need or desire to do. There are no limitations on their power.

Document 3

King Louis XIV said that the interests of the state were more important than those of the individual. The king, as head of the government, must give the orders and the subjects will carry them out as directed. It is necessary for the king to govern in this manner because it is in the best interests of the state. In addition, the people will continue to ask for more if given any voice.

Document 4

Voltaire suggested that the best government is one that protects all people—a democracy. He believed that freedom of speech is essential.

Document 5

According to Locke, governments are established to protect the natural rights of men. Governments derive their power from the governed who give their consent. Consequently, they were establishing a democratic government. Under specific conditions, such as when the government tries to assume more power at the expense of the people, the people have the right to revolt and take back the power they have given to the government.

Document 6

Montesquieu described a division of power in a basically democratic government. He stressed the importance of dividing the power so that no one branch or person has all the power, thus preventing despotism.

Additional Information Beyond the Documents

The documents provide students with only fragments of evidence. Answers should include relevant information from beyond the documents—information that students have learned from their classroom study. The following list suggests some of the information that students might include in their essays from their outside learning.

Positive and negative characteristics of the rule of monarchs such as Louis XIV in France,
    Peter the Great in Russia, Philip II in Spain, Elizabeth I in England, James I in England
Understanding of political systems of absolutism and democracy, natural rights, and other ideas
    of the Enlightenment writers Montesquieu and Voltaire

Sample Student Essay and Suggested Grading

Absolutism, which put unlimited power in the hands of the monarch, and democracy, which placed power in the hands of the people, have been important forms of government through history. Yet absolutism, in my opinion, proved to be the most effective form of government in the seventeenth and eighteenth centuries. This is supported by well known absolute monarchs King James I and King Louis XIV of France, as well as Machiavelli in *The Prince*. For the time period, absolutism was the most efficient government as decisions were made quickly so that the people had their needs met. In addition, at that time divine right rule was accepted by most people. But in the future the ideas of democracy would take hold.

First, absolute monarchies are efficient. In an absolute monarchy, there is one head, not whole groups of people to converse with about a new law or idea; therefore decisions are made quickly, and with the benefit of the state in mind. "The head alone has the right to deliberate and decide, and the functions of all the other members consist only in carrying out the commands given to them . . . The interest of the state must come first. . . ." *(Document 3)* Here King Louis of France described the positive aspects of an absolute monarch. In contrast, Montesquieu suggested that executive, legislative, and judicial powers share power. *(Document 6)* But this democratic government took too much time—the decision had to go through many people. In the seventeenth and eighteenth centuries, government could not survive the time required, but in the future centuries it would.

In addition, the absolute monarch was positive for its time period in the sense that absolute monarchs provided the people with what they needed, like roads and other public buildings and developed manufacturing. King Louis describes this through: "The interest of the state must come first." The decisions made by the absolute monarch clearly reflect a beneficial result for the people. However, in the future, a one-person decision would fail to meet the needs of the people as not only would people want a say in their government, but also wanted ". . . [to be] by nature, free, equal and independent, no one can be . . . subjected to the political power of another without his own consent." *(Document 5, Locke)*

Finally, absolute monarchs of the seventeenth and eighteenth centuries claimed their power was supreme, ". . . for kings are not only God's lieutenants . . . but even by God himself they are called gods." *(Document 2, James I)* By providing a reason for power, the people could easily be assured that the power of their ruler was genuine and they accepted it. However, this "divine right" theory created a fear among the people of the king, a positive aspect in Machiavelli's view; "Men have less hesitation in offending a man who is loved than one who is feared . . . fear is accompanied by the dread of punishment, which never relaxes." *(Document 1)* The people obeyed. However, once again, this theory would prove negative in the future, as new thinking emerged; in the writings of Voltaire, ". . . I will defend your right to say it (your opinion)." *(Document 4)* This statement defends the freedom of speech—something that the people living in the early times of monarchies knew nothing about.

In conclusion, absolutism proved an effective way of government for the seventeenth and eighteenth centuries. It provided a sense of stability, created order, and gave the people the answers and decisions needed to carry out life. But though positive then, in the future, with new age thinkers and ideas, the old ways of the absolute monarchies would fail to survive.

Teacher Comments

This student essay takes a position and supports it with evidence—providing three reasons why absolutism was the most efficient form of government for the seventeenth and eighteenth centuries. The student incorporates the documents as well as includes outside information. Structurally, the essay is well organized, with an introduction and conclusion. The essay lacks clarity due to the references to the future when the ideas of the Enlightenment and democracy will be implemented. Score: level 4.

Name_____ Date_____

Historical Context:

The Industrial Revolution refers to the greatly increased output of machine-made goods that began in England in the 1700's within the textile industry. Before the Industrial Revolution, people wove textiles by hand. Beginning in the middle of the eighteenth century, machines did this and other jobs as well. Greatly improved farming methods resulted in an agricultural revolution that paved the way for changes in manufacturing techniques. There were many reasons why the Industrial Revolution began in England and then spread to continental Europe and North America.

◆ **Directions:** The following question is based on the accompanying documents in Part A. As you analyze the documents, take into account both the source of the document and the author's point of view. Be sure to:

1. Carefully read the document-based question. Consider what you already know about this topic. How would you answer the question if you had no documents to examine?

2. Now, read each document carefully, underlining key phrases and words that address the document-based question. You may also wish to use the margin to make brief notes. Answer the questions which follow each document.

3. Based on your own knowledge and on the information found in the documents, formulate a thesis that directly answers the question.

4. Organize supportive and relevant information into a brief outline.

5. Write a well-organized essay proving your thesis. The essay should be logically presented and should include information both from the documents and from your own knowledge outside of the documents.

Question: *Why did the Industrial Revolution begin in England?*

◆ **Part A:** Examine each document carefully, and answer the questions that follow.

Document 1

England—
resources and canals—
circa 1700

(continued)

DBQ 12: The Industrial Revolution: Beginnings *(continued)*

According to the map, what resources did England have that were needed for industrialization?

_____

_____

Document 2

This excerpt is from a witness's description before the Factory Commission in 1833.

> You have been a witness of the operative [working] class in these parts; you have seen it grow from nothing into a great body in the space of a few years: how was it recruited? . . . A good many from the agricultural parts . . . People left other occupations and came to spinning for the sake of the high wages.

Why were factory workers available? _____

Document 3

The following excerpt from Adam Smith's *Wealth of Nations* written in 1776 describes the assembly line used in factories.

> I have seen a small manufactory [factory] of this kind where ten men only were employed, and where some of them performed two or three distinct operations. . . . They could . . . make among them . . . upwards of 48,000 pins in a day. . . . But if they had all wrought [worked] separately and independently . . . they certainly could not each of them have made twenty . . . in a day.

According to Smith, why were workers in a factory so productive? _____

Document 4

Here is an excerpt from *Landmarks in English Industrial History,* a book written by George Warner in 1899 (London: Blackie and Son, 1924).

> England . . . has been fortunate in possessing the natural conditions necessary to success. . . . We recognize that England is rich in these advantages, that she has coal and iron lying close together, that her sheep give the best wool, that her harbors are plentiful, that she is not ill-off for rivers, and that no part of the country is farther than seventy miles from the sea.

How did geography help England industrialize? _____

(continued)

Document-Based Assessment
Activities for Global History Classes

DBQ 12: The Industrial Revolution: Beginnings *(continued)*

Document 5

This excerpt is from *The Industrial Revolution* by Thomas S. Ashton (Oxford University Press, revised edition, 1962).

> . . . systematic thought lay behind most of the innovations in industrial practice. Invention . . . rarely thrives in a community of simple peasants or unskilled manual laborers: only when division of labor has developed . . . does it come to harvest. The stream of English scientific thought was one of the main tributaries [causes] of the industrial revolution . . . discoveries in different fields of activity were linked together. . . .

How did innovation lead to the Industrial Revolution in England? _____

_____

_____

_____

Document 6

Changes in textile machinery		
Inventor	**Invention**	**Importance**
John Kay	flying shuttle	Increased speed of weaving
James Hargreaves	spinning jenny	Spun 8–10 threads at a time; used at home
Richard Arkwright	water frame	Large spinning machine driven by water in factory
Edward Cartwright	power loom	Water powered; automatically wove thread into cloth
Eli Whitney	cotton gin	Separated seed from raw cotton

Which three inventions were most important in increasing textile production? Explain your answer.

_____

_____

_____

_____

_____

(continued)

67 *Document-Based Assessment Activities for Global History Classes*

DBQ 12: The Industrial Revolution: Beginnings *(continued)*

Document 7

Changes in agriculture		
Inventor	**Invention**	**Importance**
Jethro Tull	horse-drawn seed drill	Planted seeds in straight rows
Robert Blakewell	stock breeding	Improved quality of animals to produce more meat, milk, and wool
Cyrus McCormick	mechanical reaper	Made grain harvesting easier

What was the result of these changes in agriculture in England? _____

_____

Document 8

The following excerpt is from *The Farmer's Tour Through the East of England* by Arthur Young, 1771.

> As I shall leave Norfolk, it is proper to give a review of the farming methods which have made . . . this country so famous in the farming world. . . . The great improvements have been made by the following methods.
> By enclosing without the help of Parliament
> By the introduction of a four year rotation of crops
> By growing turnips, clover, and rye grass
> By the country being divided chiefly into large farms

How did these four changes in agriculture enable England to industrialize more easily?

_____

_____

Document 9

This excerpt is from *The Industrial and Commercial Revolutions in Great Britain During the Nineteenth Century* by L.C.A. Knowles (E. P. Dutton & Co., 1921).

> When one realizes the thousands of internal tariffs that obstructed [slowed down] traffic in Germany up to 1834 and the innumerable tolls and charges that hindered trade in France before 1789 . . . it is clear that the political and economic freedom in England was one of the causes of her industrial expansion.

What were two reasons cited by Knowles to explain industrialization in England? _____

_____

◆ **Part B—Essay**

> *Why did the Industrial Revolution begin in England?*

Document-Based Assessment
Activities for Global History Classes

Grading Key

Document 1

According to the map, England had the resources needed for industrialization. These included coal, iron, and lead. They also had wool. Canals connected the rivers to the seacoast so that products could be transported easily.

Document 2

This excerpt indicates that there were adequate workers for the factories. Workers came from rural areas since fewer workers were needed there. They also came to the cities because they wanted the "high wages."

Document 3

Adam Smith described the advantage of a factory where 10 men produced 48,000 pins in a day due to specialization of labor. Each man performed specific tasks. This was more productive than if they worked separately.

Document 4

England had the resources and conditions needed for industrialization: coal and iron; sheep with the best wool; many harbors, rivers, and seaports.

Document 5

England had the men with technical and scientific knowledge. They were able to make the necessary inventions and discoveries.

Document 6

The table shows the important inventions in textile machinery. For example, the flying shuttle increased the speed of weaving. The power loom automatically wove thread into cloth. The cotton gin separated seeds from raw cotton quickly. All these inventions increased textile production.

Document 7

The table shows important changes in agriculture. The drill and the reaper made it possible to increase food production and decrease the number of farmers needed to produce the food. Consequently, there were more workers available for factory jobs.

Document 8

Arthur Young, who traveled in England at the time, identified the following methods as responsible for the great improvement in farming: enclosing of fields, creation of larger farms, crop rotation, and the planting of crops that replenish nutrients in the soil.

Document 9

There were no internal tariffs to block trade.

Additional Information Beyond the Documents

The documents provide students with only fragments of evidence. Answers should include relevant information from beyond the documents—information that students have learned from their classroom study. The following list suggests some of the information that students might include in their essays from outside learning.

Reasons why industrialization began in England: natural resources, capital, markets, workers,
    positive governmental policies, transportation, power sources
Agricultural Revolution—Enclosure Acts
Inventions/Technology

DBQ 13: The Industrial Revolution: Effects

Historical Context:

The Industrial Revolution which began in England in the late 1700's had a wide range of positive and negative effects on the economic and social life of the people of England. These results have been interpreted from a variety of perspectives—the factory workers, the factory owners, the government, and others who observed the conditions in industrial cities at the time.

◆ **Directions:** The following question is based on the accompanying documents in Part A. As you analyze the documents, take into account both the source of the document and the author's point of view. Be sure to:

1. Carefully read the document-based question. Consider what you already know about this topic. How would you answer the question if you had no documents to examine?

2. Now, read each document carefully, underlining key phrases and words that address the document-based question. You may also wish to use the margin to make brief notes. Answer the questions which follow each document.

3. Based on your own knowledge and on the information found in the documents, formulate a thesis that directly answers the question.

4. Organize supportive and relevant information into a brief outline.

5. Write a well-organized essay proving your thesis. The essay should be logically presented and should include information both from the documents and from your own knowledge outside of the documents.

> **Question:** *Evaluate the positive and negative effects of the Industrial Revolution.*

◆ **Part A:** Analyze the following documents that describe the effects of the Industrial Revolution and answer the questions that follow.

Document 1

The following is an excerpt from William Cooper's testimony before the Sadler Committee in 1832.

> Sadler: What is your age?
> Cooper: I am eight and twenty.
> Sadler: When did you first begin to work in mills?
> Cooper: When I was ten years of age.
> Sadler: What were your usual hours of working?
> Cooper: We began at five in the morning and stopped at nine in the night.
> Sadler: What time did you have for meals?
> Cooper: We had just one period of forty minutes in the sixteen hours. That was at noon.
> Sadler: What means were taken to keep you awake and attentive?
> Cooper: At times we were frequently strapped.
> Sadler: When your hours were so long, did you have any time to attend a day school?
> Cooper: We had no time to go to day school.
> Sadler: Can you read and write?
> Cooper: I can read, but I cannot write.

(continued)

Document-Based Assessment
Activities for Global History Classes

DBQ 13: The Industrial Revolution: Effects *(continued)*

Does this testimony describe positive or negative effects of the Industrial Revolution? _____
Describe the effects of industrialization on children working in the factory. _____
_____
_____

Document 2

Here is an excerpt from the testimony of Joseph Hebergam to the Sadler Committee.

Sadler: What is the nature of your illness?
Hebergam: I have damaged lungs. My leg muscles do not function properly and will not
    support the weight of my bones.
Sadler: A doctor has told you that you will die within the year, is that correct?
Hebergam: I have been so told.
Sadler: Did he tell you the cause of your illness?
Hebergam: He told me that it was caused by the dust in the factories and from overwork and
    insufficient diet. . . .
Sadler: To what was his (your brother's) death attributed?
Hebergam: He was cut by a machine and he died of infection.
Sadler: Do you know of any other children who died at the R____ Mill?
Hebergam: There were about a dozen died during the two years and a half that I was there.
    At the L____ Mill where I worked last, a boy was caught in a machine and had both his
    thigh bones broke and from his knee to his hip the flesh was ripped up the same as it had
    been cut by a knife. His hand was bruised, his eyes were nearly torn out and his arms
    were broken. His sister, who ran to pull him off, had both her arms broke and her head
    bruised. The boy died. I do not know if the girl is dead, but she was not expected to live.
Sadler: Did the accident occur because the shaft was not covered?
Hebergam: Yes.

Does this testimony describe positive or negative effects of the Industrial Revolution?

_____

What effect did the working conditions have on the workers? _____

_____

_____

(continued)

DBQ 13: The Industrial Revolution: Effects *(continued)*

Document 3

This excerpt is from *The Philosophy of Manufactures* by Andrew Ure, 1835.

> I have visited many factories, both in Manchester and in the surrounding districts, and I never saw a single instance of corporal chastisement [beating] inflicted on a child. They seemed to be always cheerful and alert, taking pleasure in the light play of their muscles. . . . As to exhaustion, they showed no trace of it on emerging from the mill in the evening; for they began to skip about. . . . It is moreover my firm conviction [opinion] that children would thrive better when employed in our modern factories, than if left at home in apartments too often ill-aired, damp, and cold.

How does Andrew Ure describe the conditions in factories he visited? _____

_____

_____

_____

Document 4

This excerpt is from *The Working Man's Companion* subtitled *The Results of Machinery, Namely Cheap Production and Increased Employment.* It was published in 1831.

> You are surrounded, as we have constantly shown you throughout this book, with an infinite number of comforts and conveniences which had no existence two or three centuries ago and those comforts are not used only by a few, but are within the reach of almost all men. Every day is adding something to your comforts. Your houses are better built, your clothes are cheaper, you have an infinite number of domestic utensils. You can travel cheaply from place to place, and not only travel at less expense, but travel ten times quicker than two hundred years ago.

According to this author, were the effects of the Industrial Revolution positive or negative? Cite three details from the excerpt to support your answer. _____

_____

_____

_____

(continued)

DBQ 13: The Industrial Revolution: Effects *(continued)*

Document 5

This description is from a pamphlet published in 1797 by the Society for Bettering the Condition and Increasing the Comforts of the Poor.

> The village contains about 1500 inhabitants, of whom all who are capable of work are employed in and about the mills. Of these there are 500 children who are entirely fed, clothed, and educated by Mr. Dale. The others live with their parents in the village and have a weekly allowance for their work. The healthy appearance of these children has frequently attracted the attention of the traveler. Special regulations, adopted by Mr. Dale, have made this factory very different from the others in this kingdom. Out of the nearly 3000 children employed in the mills from 1785 to 1797, only fourteen have died.

What benefits were provided to people of this village? _____

_____

_____

_____

Document 6

This excerpt, from *Manchester in 1844*, was written by Leon Faucher (Frank Cass & Co. Ltd., 1969) after his visit to English factory towns.

> The little town of Hyde was at the beginning of the century a little hamlet of only 800 people, on the summit of a barren hill, the soil of which did not yield sufficient food for the inhabitants. The brothers Ashton have peopled and enriched this desert. . . . Mr. T. Ashton employs 1500 work people [in his factories]. The young women are well and decently clothed. . . . The houses inhabited by the work people form long and large streets. Mr. Ashton has built 300 of them, which he lets [rents] for . . . 75 cents per week. . . . Everywhere is to be observed a cleanliness which indicates order and comfort.

What did Leon Faucher observe when he visited Hyde? _____

_____

_____

_____

(continued)

DBQ 13: The Industrial Revolution: Effects *(continued)*

Document 7

This excerpt from *The Conditions of the Working Class in England* was written by Friedrich Engels after he visited an English industrial city in 1844.

> Every great town has one or more slum areas where the workers struggle through life as best they can out of sight of the more fortunate classes of society. The slums . . . are generally unplanned wildernesses of one- or two-storied houses. Wherever possible these have cellars which are also used as dwellings. The streets are usually unpaved, full of holes, filthy and strewn with refuse. Since they have neither gutters nor drains, the refuse accumulates in stagnant, stinking puddles. The view of Manchester is quite typical. The main river is narrow, coal-black and full of stinking filth and rubbish which it deposits on its bank. . . . One walks along a very rough path on the river bank to reach a chaotic group of little, one-story, one-room cabins. . . . In front of the doors, filth and garbage abounded. . . .

What did Engels observe as he visited an English industrial city? _____

_____

Why did Engels focus on the negative results of industrialization? _____

_____

_____

Document 8

This table shows:

British Iron Production (1740–1900)	
1740	17,350 tons
1796	125,079 tons
1839	1,248,781 tons
1854	3,100,000 tons
1900	9,000,000 tons

Describe British iron production between 1740–1900. _____

_____

Is this a positive or negative effect of the Industrial Revolution? Explain. _____

_____

◆ **Part B—Essay**

> *Evaluate the positive and negative effects of the Industrial Revolution.*

Grading Key

Document 1

The testimony before the Sadler Committee provided information on child labor—William Cooper began work at age 10. He worked 16 hours a day with no time for school. The information is from the perspective of a person who worked in a factory and describes negative effects.

Document 2

This testimony before the Sadler Committee discusses injuries and deaths due to unsafe machines at the factories. The dust in the factories, as well as overwork, led to damaged lungs for Joseph Hebergam. This description is a negative effect of industrialization.

Document 3

In contrast to prior documents, Andrew Ure claimed to have visited many factories near Manchester where he saw happy children happily working. They are not exhausted after their work in the mill; rather they skipped home. In fact, Ure feels they are better off employed in the modern factories than at home in damp, cold apartments.

Document 4

According to this author, most people had more comfortable lives with better homes, cheaper clothing, and easier travel.

Document 5

This description of a model factory town describes how Mr. Dale provided for the care and education of 500 children who are employed in his mills. Mr. Dale's regulations ensured that the children were healthy and, as a result, only 14 had died in the 12 years prior to the study.

Document 6

The author described the town of Hyde, which he visited in 1844. In this town Mr. Ashton, the factory owner, provided for his workers. He built houses that were rented to workers for 75 cents a week. The houses were very pleasant. As a result, everything seemed to be clean and orderly in this town which, otherwise, was a barren wasteland.

Document 7

When Friedrich Engels visited Manchester, an English industrial city, in 1844, he found exactly the opposite conditions. The city had a slum area where the workers lived. Here the unpaved, filthy garbage-strewn streets were full of holes and stagnant water. The river was black with garbage floating on it. The houses were one-room shacks. Engels, who favored socialism, saw only negative results of industrialism.

Document 8

British iron production increased rapidly from 17,350 tons in 1740 to 1,248,781 tons in 1839, and continued to rise. This is evidence of the industrialization of Britain.

Additional Information Beyond the Documents

The documents provide students with only fragments of evidence. Answers should include relevant information from beyond the documents—information that students have learned from their classroom study. The following list suggests some of the information that students might include in their essays from outside learning.

The positive and negative effects of industrialization

Increased productivity—mass production, growing middle class of factory owners, merchants, and shippers whose wealth increases, growth of industrial cities, unsafe working conditions in factories, pollution

DBQ 14: The Industrial Revolution: Responses

Historical Context:

The impact of the Industrial Revolution was a positive experience for some, but for others it was a time of great difficulty. Consequently, demands for reform and protection for workers arose. Governments and unions began to take action. Others advocated the overthrow of the capitalist system because of its inherent evils. They suggested socialism.

◆ **Directions:** The following question is based on the accompanying documents in Part A. As you analyze the documents, take into account both the source of the document and the author's point of view. Be sure to:

1. Carefully read the document-based question. Consider what you already know about this topic. How would you answer the question if you had no documents to examine?

2. Now, read each document carefully, underlining key phrases and words that address the document-based question. You may also wish to use the margin to make brief notes. Answer the questions which follow each document.

3. Based on your own knowledge and on the information found in the documents, formulate a thesis that directly answers the question.

4. Organize supportive and relevant information into a brief outline.

5. Write a well-organized essay proving your thesis. The essay should be logically presented and should include information both from the documents and from your own knowledge outside of the documents.

> **Question:** *How were the evils of the Industrial Revolution addressed in England in the eighteenth and nineteenth centuries?*

◆ **Part A:** Analyze the following documents that describe responses to the evils of the Industrial Revolution and answer the questions that follow.

Document 1

This excerpt is from the Combination Act of 1800, which hindered the growth of unions.

> . . . that every workman . . . who shall . . . enter into any combination [union] to obtain an advance of wages, or to lessen or alter the hours . . . or who shall, for the purpose of obtaining an advance in wages . . . persuade, solicit, intimidate, or influence . . . any workman . . . to quit or leave his work . . . shall be committed to . . . jail. . . .

How did the Combination Act of 1800 hinder the growth of unions? _____

_____

_____

_____

(continued)

DBQ 14: The Industrial Revolution: Responses *(continued)*

Document 2

This excerpt, from "Solidarity Forever" by Ralph Chaplin, expresses his ideas about unions.

> When the union's inspiration through the workers' blood shall run,
> There can be no power greater anywhere beneath the sun.
> Yet what force on earth is weaker than the feeble strength of one?
> But the union makes us strong.

According to this song, why should a worker join the union? _____

_____

_____

Document 3

This excerpt is from the Health and Morals Act of 1802.

> The minimum age of employment shall be nine years.
> The working day for children under fourteen shall be limited to twelve hours.

What reform did this government legislation make? _____

_____

_____

Document 4

This excerpt is from the Factory Act of 1833.

> Be it enacted that no person under 18 years of age shall be allowed to work in the night in
> or about any cotton, woolen, linen, or silk mill or factory, where steam, water, or any other
> mechanical power is used to work the machinery . . . no person under the age of 18 years
> shall be employed in any such mill or factory more than 12 hours in one day, nor more than
> 69 hours in any one week . . . his majesty [the king of England] shall appoint . . . inspectors
> of factories . . . where the labor of children under 18 years of age is employed.

How did the Factory Act of 1833 affect child labor? _____

_____

_____

(continued)

Document-Based Assessment
Activities for Global History Classes

DBQ 14: The Industrial Revolution: Responses *(continued)*

Document 5

The following excerpt is from Adam Smith's *The Wealth of Nations*, 1776.

> The sole purpose of all production is to provide the best possible goods to the consumer at the lowest possible price. Society should assist producers of goods and services only to the extent that assisting them benefits the consumer . . . he intends his own gain; and he is in this, as in many other cases, led by an invisible hand to promote an end which was no part of his intention . . . By pursuing his own interest, he frequently promotes that of the society. . . .

According to Adam Smith, what should the role of the government be in the economy?

_____

_____

_____

Document 6

This excerpt is from the Chartist petition to Parliament in 1838.

> May it please your honorable house, to take our petition into your most serious consideration and . . . to have a law passed, granting to every male of lawful age . . . the right of voting for members of parliament, and . . . elections of members of parliaments to be by secret ballot. . . .

What were two changes suggested by the Chartists? _____

_____

_____

(continued)

Document-Based Assessment
Activities for Global History Classes

DBQ 14: The Industrial Revolution: Responses *(continued)*

Document 7

This excerpt is from the *Condition of the Working Class in England in 1844* by Friedrich Engels. In it he criticizes capitalism.

> People regard each other only as useful objects; each exploits the other, and the end of it all is, that the stronger treads the weaker under foot, and that the powerful few, the capitalists, seize everything for themselves, while to the weak . . . the poor, scarcely a bare existence remains.

What are Engels' criticisms of capitalism? _____

_____

_____

Document 8

Here is an excerpt from the *Communist Manifesto* written by Marx and Engels in 1848.

> The Communists . . . openly declare that their ends can be attained [gained] only by the forcible overthrow of all existing social conditions. Let the ruling classes tremble at a communist revolution. The proletarians have nothing to lose but their chains. They have a world to win. Working men of all countries, unite!

What solution to the evils of capitalism did Marx and Engels recommend? _____

_____

_____

◆ Part B—Essay

> *How were the evils of the Industrial Revolution addressed in England in the eighteenth and nineteenth centuries?*

 Document-Based Assessment
Activities for Global History Classes

Grading Key

Document 1

According to the Combination Act of 1800, anyone who joined a union to get higher wages or shorter work hours or tried to get fellow workers to stop work was engaged in illegal activities and could be sent to jail. This hindered the growth of unions.

Document 2

This song urged workers to join the union, for there would be strength in numbers—in union membership.

Document 3

In 1802, a law was passed that set the minimum age for workers at 9 years of age. The workday was limited to 12 hours for children under 14 years of age.

Document 4

In 1833, the Factory Act set conditions of employment for workers under 18 years of age and provided for inspectors in factories employing children under 18. It said that no person under 18 years of age could work in a textile factory powered by mechanical power at night or for more than 12 hours a day.

Document 5

Adam Smith, an advocate of laissez-faire capitalism, suggested that if producers freely pursue their own gain or interest, the economy and society will benefit along with the producer. Social harmony would result without government intervention. This would happen naturally, as if by an "invisible hand."

Document 6

In this petition to Parliament, the Chartists suggested all males have the right to vote. They also suggested a secret ballot be used in the elections for Parliament.

Document 7

Engels, coauthor of the *Communist Manifesto*, pointed out the evils of capitalism that came with the Industrial Revolution. He saw the powerful few, the capitalists, exploiting or taking advantage of the weaker workers for their own profit.

Document 8

In the *Communist Manifesto*, Marx and Engels predicted that the workers would join in a communist revolution. They would overthrow capitalism and establish a more equitable society through communism.

Additional Information Beyond the Documents

The documents provide students with only fragments of evidence. Answers should include relevant information from beyond the documents—information that students have learned from their classroom study. The following list suggests some of the information that students might include in their essays from outside learning.

Adam Smith and laissez-faire capitalism

Karl Marx and scientific socialism, *Communist Manifesto*

Unionization and legislative reforms by English government

DBQ 15: Nationalism in the Nineteenth Century

Historical Context:

Nationalism was the most powerful force in the 1800's. Beginning with the French Revolution of 1789, nationalism contributed to the unification of Italy and Germany in the nineteenth century. At the same time, ethnic unrest threatened to topple the Ottoman and the Austro-Hungarian empires. Nationalism also contributed to the outbreak of wars such as the Franco-Prussian War and World War I.

◆ **Directions:** The following question is based on the accompanying documents in Part A. As you analyze the documents, take into account both the source of the document and the author's point of view. Be sure to:

1. Carefully read the document-based question. Consider what you already know about this topic. How would you answer the question if you had no documents to examine?
2. Now, read each document carefully, underlining key phrases and words that address the document-based question. You may also wish to use the margin to make brief notes. Answer the questions which follow each document.
3. Based on your own knowledge and on the information found in the documents, formulate a thesis that directly answers the question.
4. Organize supportive and relevant information into a brief outline.
5. Write a well-organized essay proving your thesis. The essay should be logically presented and should include information both from the documents and from your own knowledge outside of the documents.

> **Question:** *Nationalism united people into nation-states, toppled empires composed of many ethnic minorities, and contributed to the outbreak of wars in the nineteenth century. How would you evaluate this statement?*

◆ **Part A:** Analyze the following documents that provide information about nationalism as a force in nineteenth-century Europe and answer the questions that follow.

Document 1

This excerpt is from the *Levée en Masse,* French Revolution, August 23, 1793.

> The young men shall go forth to battle; the married men will make arms and transport food; the women will make tents, uniforms, and will serve in the hospitals; the children will prepare lint from old linens; the old men will gather in public places to raise the courage of the warriors, to excite hatred of kings and to preach the unity of the Republic.

What was the impact on the French of the *Levée en Masse?* _____

_____

_____

_____

(continued)

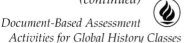

DBQ 15: Nationalism in the Nineteenth Century (continued)

Document 2

The "Marseillaise," the French national anthem, arouses the emotions of the French during the revolution. They must fight for their country.

> Arise, children of the fatherland,
> Our day of glory has arrived.
> Against us cruel tyrants
> Have raised their bloody flag.
> Do you hear in the countryside
> Their fierce hired soldiers?
> They come almost into your arms
> To attack your children and your fields.
> *Chorus:* To arms, citizens!
> Form your battalions!
> March on, march on,
> To liberty or death!

What did the national anthem urge the French to do? _____

_____

Document 3

This excerpt is from Count Cavour who was named prime minister of Piedmont-Sardinia in 1852. As a diplomat, he provided the "brains" of Italian unification.

> We ardently wish to free Italy from foreign rule. . . . We want to drive out the foreigners not only because we want to see our country powerful and glorious, but because we want to elevate the Italian people in intelligence and moral development.

What action did Cavour recommend in this excerpt? _____

_____

Document 4

Giuseppe Garibaldi, the "sword" of Italian unification, added the southern Kingdom of the Two Sicilies to Italy in 1861. He describes his "Red Shirts" with these words.

> O noble Thousand! . . . I love to remember you! . . . Where any of our brothers are fighting for liberty, there all Italians must hasten!—such was your motto. Let him who loves his country in his heart, and not with his lips only, follow me.

What is Garabaldi trying to accomplish in this speech? _____

_____

(continued)

DBQ 15: Nationalism in the Nineteenth Century *(continued)*

Document 5

These words were spoken by Otto von Bismarck, who some people feel single-handedly unified Germany and started it on its road to greatness. He explains the process for unification of Germany.

> I had shown plainly the direction in which I was going. Prussia . . . could no longer carry alone the power that Germany required for its security. That must be equally distributed over all German peoples. We would get not nearer our goal by speeches, associations, or decisions by the majority. We would not be able to avoid serious contest with Austria. This contest could only be settled by blood and iron. There is one way to guarantee our success. The deputies must place the greatest possible weight of blood and iron in the hands of the King of Prussia.

Describe Bismarck's method for uniting Germany. _____

_____

_____

Document 6

In this excerpt, Princip, the assassin of Archduke Franz Ferdinand in 1914, explains his motives.

> . . . I am a nationalist. I aimed to free the Yugoslavs. For I am a Yugoslav. . . . As far as Serbia is concerned, it is her duty to free us.

Who does Princep say he is and what is he doing? _____

_____

_____

_____

(continued)

DBQ 15: Nationalism in the Nineteenth Century *(continued)*

Document 7

This illustration shows the effect of nationalism among the subject nationalities of the Austro-Hungarian Empire.

What does this illustration show is the effect of nationalism on the Austrian Empire? _____

_____

_____

_____

◆ **Part B—Essay**

> *Nationalism united people into nation-states, toppled empires composed of many ethnic minorities, and contributed to the outbreak of wars in the nineteenth century. How would you evaluate this statement?*

Grading Key

Document 1

Everyone had a role to play as the French united to fight against the other European countries who were attacking France.

Document 2

This national anthem urged the people to unite for the fatherland against the cruel tyrants and their mercenary soldiers. The French must take up arms and march together for "liberty or death." This is an emotional call to action and unity.

Document 3

Cavour, the politician, believed the Italians must get rid of foreign controlling countries, like Austria, in order to unite Italy. He was a leader of Italian unification.

Document 4

Garibaldi, another leader of Italian unification, saw the importance of military action as he motivated his "Red Shirts" to fight for liberty out of love for their country.

Document 5

Bismarck, a nationalist, said that Prussia needed the support of all Germans in the unification movement. Furthermore, they must use war—"blood and iron"—to unite the country under Prussian leadership.

Document 6

Princep, the assassin of the archduke, said he was a nationalist who was fighting to free and unite the Yugoslavs.

Document 7

The cartoon shows that nationalism was blowing apart the Austrian Empire because its subject nationalities want their own countries.

Additional Information Beyond the Documents

The documents provide students with only fragments of evidence. Answers should include relevant information from beyond the documents—information that students have learned from their classroom study. The following list suggests some of the information that students might include in their essays from outside learning.

Nationalist leaders, their methods, and events that resulted in the unification of Germany and Italy

The Austrian and Ottoman empires and the demands of their ethnic groups for independence
   (for example, Yugoslavia today)

Wars caused by nationalism—World War I, World War II
                    Franco Prussian War

Sample Student Essay and Suggested Grading

Nationalism, which began in the 1800's through the events of the French Revolution, became a powerful force in Europe in the later nineteenth century. As it grew, nationalism united people in countries of Germany and Italy. Yet it also divided the Ottoman and Austro-Hungarian empires and led to the outbreak of wars.

Unification occurred as a result of nationalism, which developed between groups of people of similar culture, religion, language, and traditions. During the French Revolution nationalism was evident in the *Levée en masse* ". . . young men shall go forth to battle . . ., women will make tents . . . old men will gather in public places to raise the courage of the warriors . . ." *(Document 1)* to fight a common enemy for common goals. The French national anthem *(Document 2)* also encouraged them to fight together. A similar feeling spread to Germany and Italy. In Germany, nationalism was encouraged by Otto von Bismarck, nicknamed the "iron chancellor." He believed that uniting Germany had to occur with ". . . blood and iron . . ." *(Document 5)* Bismarck disliked passive ways of decision making like speeches or voting; rather he wanted to fight, and provoke war, as he did with Austria in the Seven Weeks War, and France in the Franco-Prussian War. With blood and iron he united Germany, either by winning the land in war or through creating nationalism, which joined independent states to form the whole country. In Italy, prime minister Count Cavour, who provided the brains and acted as diplomat of Italian unification stated, "We wish to free Italy from foreign rule. We want to drive out the foreigners . . . because we want to elevate the Italian people in intelligence and moral development." *(Document 3)* Because of the separate Italian states and its partial rule by the Austrian Empire, the Italians were very much separated. Yet, as nationalism grew, the Italian people came together as a whole to free the areas in the north and south from foreign rule. Giuseppe Garibaldi, the "sword" of unification, helped bring southern Italy to complete unification with his Red Shirts. He said, "Where any of our brothers are fighting for liberty, all Italians must hasten!" *(Document 4)* Nationalism grew, so that like Germany, the states came together as the whole country of Italy.

However, nationalism also caused disunification, by creating wars and breaking up empires. As in the Austro-Hungarian Empire, there were many different ethnic groups, as shown in a cartoon in Document 7. Nationalism separated these people and they soon demanded to be separate nation-states. The Austrian Empire declined as the Hungarians, who made up a majority of the empire, demanded a say in government; the empire was then called the Austro-Hungarian Empire. Soon the other groups in the empire developed nationalism and wanted their own countries. "I am a nationalist. I aimed to free the Yugoslavs. For I am a Yugoslav. . . ." said a Serb. *(Document 6)* World War I brought the end of this once powerful Austrian Empire. A similar situation occurred within the Ottoman Empire. After Suleiman the Great died, a line of very weak sultans followed, which weakened the empire as nationalism grew among the mixed ethnic groups, leading to the Balkan War. The Ottomans were too weak to maintain order. Revolution, beginning with the Greeks' war for independence in 1830, was followed by other ethnic unrest so that by the end of World War I, the Ottoman Empire had been destroyed.

However, wars also resulted from nationalism. Wars not only ended in disunification, as the Balkan War weakened the Ottoman Empire, but they also were used in unification—von Bismarck's Seven Weeks War and the Franco-Prussian War brought together the German states. Also, the Italians, fought their way to unification of the northern and southern foreign-dominated areas through wars.

In conclusion, nationalism was a driving force in both the unification and disunification of countries and empires in Europe. Nationalism can obviously be assumed to be one of the most powerful movements in history, for it helped in creating the countries and cultures that we know or even descend from today.

Teacher Comments

This essay addresses all aspects of the task. It describes how nationalism united Italy and Germany as well as dividing the Ottoman and Austro-Hungarian empires with wars. It integrates outside information with information from documents. The essay is well organized and has a strong introduction and conclusion. Score: level 5.

Name_____ Date_____

Historical Context:

Between 1870 and 1920, European imperialism accelerated due to economic, political, and social forces. The Industrial Revolution stirred the ambitions of European nations, and with the advances in technology, these nations were able to spread their control over the less-developed areas of the world. This empire-building frenzy has been studied by historians who offer a variety of perspectives on its causes.

◆ **Directions:** The following question is based on the accompanying documents in Part A. As you analyze the documents, take into account both the source of the document and the author's point of view. Be sure to:

1. Carefully read the document-based question. Consider what you already know about this topic. How would you answer the question if you had no documents to examine?

2. Now, read each document carefully, underlining key phrases and words that address the document-based question. You may also wish to use the margin to make brief notes. Answer the questions which follow each document.

3. Based on your own knowledge and on the information found in the documents, formulate a thesis that directly answers the question.

4. Organize supportive and relevant information into a brief outline.

5. Write a well-organized essay proving your thesis. The essay should be logically presented and should include information both from the documents and from your own knowledge outside of the documents.

> **Question:** *Which economic, political, and social forces were most responsible for the new imperialism that began in the late nineteenth and twentieth centuries?*

◆ **Part A:** The following documents provide information about the causes for the new imperialism. Examine the documents carefully, and answer the questions that follow.

Document 1

This excerpt is from *Imperialism and World Politics,* written by Parker T. Moon. He points out which groups were most interested in imperialism.

The makers of cotton and iron goods have been very much interested in imperialism. This group of import interests has been greatly strengthened by the demand of giant industries for colonial raw materials. . . . Shipowners demand coaling stations for their vessels and naval bases for protection. To these interests may be added the makers of armaments and of uniforms. The producers of telegraph and railway material and other supplies used by the government in its colony may also be included. . . . Finally the most powerful business groups are the bankers. Banks make loans to colonies and backward countries for building railways and steamship lines. . . .

(continued)

Document-Based Assessment
Activities for Global History Classes

DBQ 16: New Imperialism: Causes *(continued)*

Which groups are seeking colonies according to this author? Explain each group's reason.

_____

_____

_____

Document 2

This excerpt was written by the American Senator A. J. Beveridge in 1898.

> American factories are making more than the American people can use; American soil is producing more than they can consume. Fate has written our policy for us; the trade of the world must and shall be ours. . . . We will establish trading posts throughout the world as distributing points for American products. We will cover the ocean with our merchant marines. We will build a navy to the measure of our greatness. . . .

According to Senator Beveridge, why should America become imperialistic? _____

_____

Document 3

This excerpt, from Raymond Aron's book *The Century of Total War*, suggests another cause for imperialism.

> . . . none of the colonial undertakings was motivated by the quest for capitalist profits; they all originated in political ambitions . . . the nations' will to power . . . glory or national greatness.

What does this author say was the cause for imperialism? _____

_____

Document 4

Cecil Rhodes, a successful British imperialist in Africa, expresses his position in *Confession of Faith*, written in 1877.

> I contend that we [Britons] are the finest race in the world, and the more of the world we inhabit, the better it is for the human race. . . . It is our duty to seize every opportunity of acquiring more territory and we should keep this one idea steadily before our eyes that more territory simply means more of the Anglo-Saxon race, more of the best, the most human, most honourable race the world possesses.

What does Cecil Rhodes believe is the reason for imperialism? _____

_____

(continued)

DBQ 16: New Imperialism: Causes *(continued)*

Document 5

In the excerpt from William L. Langer's book, *The Diplomacy of Imperialism*, another reason is suggested.

> But the economic side . . . must not be allowed to obscure [hide] the other factors. Psychologically speaking . . . evolutionary teaching [about the "survival of the fittest"] was perhaps most crucial. It not only justified competition and struggle but introduced an element of ruthlessness. . . .

According to Langer, what was the reason for the new imperialism? _____

_____

_____

Document 6

In this excerpt from Rudyard Kipling's *The White Man's Burden*, there is another explanation for imperialism.

> Take up the white man's burden
> send forth the best ye breed
> Go bind your sons to exile
> To serve your captives' need,
> To wait, in heavy harness,
> On fluttered folk and wild
> Your new caught, sullen peoples,
> Half-devil and half-child.

According to the poem, what is the "white man's burden"? _____

_____

_____

Document 7

In this excerpt, President William McKinley explains why the United States took over the Philippines.

> We could not leave them to themselves. They were unfit for self-government. There was nothing left for us to do but to take them over. Then we would be able to educate the Filipinos. We could uplift and civilize and Christianize them. . . .

How does President McKinley explain the U.S. takeover of the Philippines? _____

_____

_____

(continued)

DBQ 16: New Imperialism: Causes (continued)

Document 8

This excerpt gives another reason why Europeans could increase their colonies. This is from a letter sent by Phan Thanh Gian, governor of a Vietnamese state, to his administrators in 1867.

> Now, the French are come, with their powerful weapons of war to cause dissension among us. We are weak against them; our commanders and our soldiers have been vanquished. . . . The French have immense warships, filled with soldiers and armed with huge cannons. No one can resist them. They go where they want, the strongest ramparts fall before them.

How does this Vietnamese man explain the French imperialism in Indochina in 1867? _____

_____

Document 9

Imperialism in Africa in 1914

Legend:
- British
- French
- Belgian
- German
- Portuguese
- Italian
- Spanish
- Independent

What cause for imperialism is evident in this map of Africa? Explain._____

_____

◆ **Part B—Essay**

> *Which economic, political, and social forces were most responsible for the new imperialism that began in the late nineteenth and early twentieth centuries?*

Grading Key

Document 1

The author pointed out many economic causes for imperialism. Specifically, he pointed to the producers of cotton and iron who needed markets; the importers who could provide raw materials to the industries; the shipowners who would need fueling stations, and the weaponsmakers and others who supplied the government. Finally, the bankers who made loans to colonies for building of railroads and other services wanted colonies. These groups benefited from imperialism.

Document 2

Senator Beveridge suggested that the United States was destined to expand its trading because it was producing so much. Also, he suggested that it would be a sign of American power if we built a merchant marine and trading empire.

Document 3

According to Aron, economics (profit) was not the cause of imperialism; rather, the cause of imperialism was political. Countries were motivated by nationalism—a desire for power and glory.

Document 4

Rhodes believed that the British were a superior race and it was their duty to acquire as much land as possible. As a result, there would be more Anglo-Saxons, the best race, controlling the world. This is a racist cause for imperialism.

Document 5

Langer said economic forces should not hide the other factors that caused imperialism. He pointed to Social Darwinism—the survival of the fittest—as the reason the Europeans were able to take over.

Document 6

According to the poem, it is the white man's burden to help care for the "half-devil and half-child," Kipling's description of the people in the colonies. The poem illustrates the racial superiority that some white people felt at that time in history.

Document 7

President McKinley said it was our responsibility to educate, uplift, civilize, and Christianize the Filipinos because they were "unfit" to rule themselves. This is another example of the racist viewpoint.

Document 8

This Vietnamese leader believed that the French were able to colonize the area because they had superior weapons and ships.

Document 9

This map shows how the Europeans (French, British, Belgians, Germans, Italians, Portuguese, and Spanish) carved up Africa. It shows the power of the Europeans.

Additional Information Beyond the Documents

The documents provide students with only fragments of evidence. Answers should include relevant information from beyond the documents—information that students have learned from their classroom study. The following list suggests some of the information that students might include in their essays from outside learning.

Maps of Africa and Asia before and after imperialism
Conditions in Europe that led to imperialism—the Industrial Revolution, missionaries, etc.
Political, social, and economic conditions in Africa and Asia before the Europeans arrived

DBQ 17: Imperialism in India: An Evaluation

Historical Context:

European imperialism in the late nineteenth and twentieth centuries resulted in the carving up of areas of Africa and Asia into vast colonial empires. This was the case for British colonialism in India. As imperialism spread, the colonizer and the colony viewed imperialism differently. They saw both positive and negative effects of imperialism.

◆ **Directions:** The following question is based on the accompanying documents in Part A. As you analyze the documents, take into account both the source of the document and the author's point of view. Be sure to:

1. Carefully read the document-based question. Consider what you already know about this topic. How would you answer the question if you had no documents to examine?

2. Now, read each document carefully, underlining key phrases and words that address the document-based question. You may also wish to use the margin to make brief notes. Answer the questions which follow each document.

3. Based on your own knowledge and on the information found in the documents, formulate a thesis that directly answers the question.

4. Organize supportive and relevant information into a brief outline.

5. Write a well-organized essay proving your thesis. The essay should be logically presented and should include information both from the documents and from your own knowledge outside of the documents.

> **Question:** *What were the positive and negative effects of imperialism for the British, the mother country, and for India, the colony?*

◆ **Part A:** The following documents provide information about the effects of imperialism on India. Examine the documents carefully, and answer the questions that follow.

Document 1

In this excerpt, adapted from O. P. Austin's "Does Colonization Pay?" in *The Forum*, January 1900, positive and negative results of imperialism are pointed out.

> Modern progressive nations [European colonizers] . . . seek to control "garden spots" in the tropics. Under their direction, these places can yield the tropical produce that their citizens need. In return the progressive nations bring to the people of those garden spots the food-stuffs, and manufactures they need. They develop the territory by building roads, canals, railways, and telegraphs. The progressive nations can establish schools and newspapers for the people of the colonies. They can also give these people the benefit of other blessings of civilization which they have not the means of creating themselves.

According to this author, what are the benefits of imperialism to the colony? _____

_____

What are the benefits of imperialism to the colonizer? _____

_____

(continued)

DBQ 17: Imperialism in India: An Evaluation *(continued)*

Document 2

In this speech, Dadabhai Naoroji, an Indian, describes the effect of imperialism on India.

> To sum up the whole, the British rule has been—morally, a great blessing; politically peace and order on one hand . . . on the other, materially, impoverishment. . . . The natives call the British system . . . "the knife of sugar." That is to say there is no oppression, it is all smooth and sweet, but it is the knife, nevertheless.

In later comments he stresses the negative aspects.

> Europeans [the British] occupy almost all the higher places in every department of government. . . . Natives, no matter how fit, are deliberately kept out of the social institutions started by Europeans. . . . All they [the Europeans] do is live off of India while they are here. When they go, they carry all they have gained.

How is British imperialism both positive and negative for India? _____

_____

_____

_____

Document 3

This excerpt is adapted from *The Economic History of India Under Early British Rule,* by an Indian, Romesh Dutt.

> Englishmen . . . have given the people of India the greatest human blessing—peace. They have introduced Western education. This has brought an ancient and civilized nation in touch with modern thought, modern sciences, and modern life. They have built an administration that is strong and efficient. They have framed wise laws and have established courts of justice.

What benefits did India gain during British imperialism? _____

_____

_____

_____

(continued)

Document-Based Assessment
Activities for Global History Classes

DBQ 17: Imperialism in India: An Evaluation *(continued)*

Document 4

This excerpt is adapted from British historian, J. A. R. Marriott's book, *The English in India*, 1932.

> British brains, British enterprise, and British capital have changed the face of India. Means of communication have been developed. There are great numbers of bridges, more than 40,000 miles of railway, and 70,000 miles of paved roads. These testify to the skill and industry of British engineers. Irrigation works on a very large scale have brought 30 million acres under cultivation. This has greatly added to the agricultural wealth of the country. Industrialization has also begun. India now has improved sanitation and a higher standard of living. It has a fine transport system and carefully thought-out schemes for relief work. Because of these things famines have now almost disappeared.

List at least five benefits of imperialism cited by this author. _____

_____

_____

_____

_____

_____

Document 5

This excerpt, from *India: A Restatement* by British writer Sir Reginald Coupland, points out the social and economic impact of imperialism on India.

> British rule brought with it from the West certain standards of humanity that Indian society had not yet reached. Early action was taken to stop infanticide [the killing of girl babies]. . . . The slave trade was ended and the owning of slaves was forbidden. . . . One result of the new order was a steady rise in the value of India's export trade.

What are the benefits of imperialism identified by this author? _____

_____

_____

_____

_____

(continued)

DBQ 17: Imperialism in India: An Evaluation *(continued)*

Document 6

This excerpt, from *The Discovery of India* by Jawaharlal Nehru, explains how India became a "typical" colonial economy.

> This process continued throughout the nineteenth century. Other old Indian industries—shipbuilding, metalwork, glass, paper—and many crafts were broken up. Thus the economic development of India was stopped and the growth of new industry was prevented. . . . A typical colonial economy was built up. India became an agricultural colony of industrial England. It supplied raw materials and provided markets for England's industrial goods. The destruction of industry led to unemployment on a vast scale. . . . The poverty of the country grew. The standard of living fell to terribly low levels.

What negative effects of imperialism does Nehru point out? _____

_____

_____

_____

Document 7

Mohandas Gandhi offers a complaint about imperialism.

> You English committed one supreme crime against my people. For a hundred years you have done everything for us. You have given us no responsibility for our own government.

What is Gandhi's criticism of imperialism? _____

_____

_____

_____

◆ **Part B—Essay**

> *What were the positive and negative effects of imperialism for the British, the mother country, and for India, the colony?*

Grading Key

Document 1

The colony benefited from imperialism because it received food and manufactured goods. Roads, canals, railways, and schools are additional "blessings of civilization" that the colony receives. The colonizer received tropical produce from the "garden spot."

Document 2

This Indian speaker referred to the British colonial rule as a "knife of sugar." India enjoyed peace and order but they suffered from material poverty. In the second extract, the author pointed out that the British held all the high government positions and lived off of India.

Document 3

This Indian, Romesh Dutt, pointed out several benefits enjoyed by India—Western education and modern science. The British also built a governmental bureaucracy that was efficient and provided law and order as well as a judicial system.

Document 4

This author believed that British money and brains brought many benefits—communication and transportation systems and an irrigation system that increased farmland and agricultural production. India also had an improved sanitary system and a social welfare system. As a result of British rule, Indians enjoyed a higher standard of living.

Document 5

This British author identified the "standards of humanity" that the British brought to India. These included the end of female infanticide, slavery, and slave trade.

Document 6

Nehru points out the negative effects for India of being a "colonial economy" for the British. Indian economic development was disrupted when the British broke up old Indian industries. India supplied raw materials and agricultural products for England, and India was a market for British industrial products. As a result of imperialism, unemployment and poverty rose in India.

Document 7

Gandhi complained that Indians were not allowed to develop the skills needed for self-government.

Additional Information Beyond the Documents

The documents provide students with only fragments of evidence. Answers should include relevant information from beyond the documents—information that students have learned from their classroom study. The following list suggests some of the information that students might include in their essays from outside learning.

Conditions in India before and during British imperialism
Reasons for opposition to imperialism

Name_____ Date_____

DBQ 18: Imperialism in Africa: An Evaluation

Historical Context:

European imperialism in the late nineteenth and twentieth centuries resulted in the carving up of areas of Africa and Asia into vast colonial empires. This was true for most of the continent of Africa. As imperialism spread, the colonizer and the colony viewed imperialism differently. They saw both positive and negative effects of imperialism.

◆ **Directions:** The following question is based on the accompanying documents in Part A. As you analyze the documents, take into account both the source of the document and the author's point of view. Be sure to:

1. Carefully read the document-based question. Consider what you already know about this topic. How would you answer the question if you had no documents to examine?

2. Now, read each document carefully, underlining key phrases and words that address the document-based question. You may also wish to use the margin to make brief notes. Answer the questions which follow each document.

3. Based on your own knowledge and on the information found in the documents, formulate a thesis that directly answers the question.

4. Organize supportive and relevant information into a brief outline.

5. Write a well-organized essay proving your thesis. The essay should be logically presented and should include information both from the documents and from your own knowledge outside of the documents.

> **Question:** *Evaluate the new imperialism of the late nineteenth and early twentieth centuries in Africa. What were the positive and negative effects of imperialism for the colonizer and the colony?*

◆ **Part A:** The following documents provide information about the effects of imperialism on Africa. Examine the documents carefully, and answer the questions that follow.

Document 1

This excerpt is adapted from *Imperialism* by J. A. Hobson, a British scholar.

> The period of imperialism has witnessed many wars. Most of these wars have been caused by attacks of white races upon so-called "lower races." They have resulted in the taking of territory by force. . . . The white rulers of the colonies live at the expense of the natives. Their chief work is to organize labor for their support. In the typical colony, the most fertile lands and the mineral resources are owned by white foreigners. These holdings are worked by natives under their direction. The foreigners take wealth out of the country. All the hard work is done by natives.

What negative aspects of imperialism does this British scholar point out? _____

_____

_____

(continued)

Document-Based Assessment
Activities for Global History Classes

DBQ 18: Imperialism in Africa: An Evaluation(continued)

Document 2

Sekou Toure, an African nationalist, pointed out another negative aspect of imperialism.

Colonialism's greatest misdeed was to have tried to strip us of our responsibility in conducting our own affairs and convince us that our civilization was nothing less than savagery, thus giving us complexes which led to our being branded as irresponsible and lacking in self-confidence.

What criticism of imperialism does this African offer? _____

_____

Document 3

The resolution of the All-African People's Conference, held in Accra, Ghana in 1958, "condemns colonialism and imperialism" based on these premises.

Whereas all African peoples . . . deplore the economic exploitation of African people by Imperialist Countries, thus reducing Africans to poverty in the midst of plenty . . . Whereas fundamental human rights, freedom of speech, freedom of association, freedom of movement, freedom of worship, freedom to live a full and abundant life . . . are denied to Africans through the activities of Imperialists.

What are the reasons this group condemned imperialism? _____

_____

Document 4

George H. T. Kimble, in a 1962 *New York Times Magazine* article, "Colonialism: the Good, the Bad, the Lessons," gives his point of view.

. . . they [the colonial powers] failed to provide the African with sufficient [preparation] . . . None of the newly independent countries had enough skilled African administrators to run their own . . . [or] enough African technicians to keep the public utilities working. . . . And no country had an electorate that knew what independence was all about. . . . For all its faults, colonial government provided security of person and property in lands that had known little of either. . . . It was the colonial powers who were largely responsible for the opening of the region to the lumberman, miner, planter, and other men of means without whom its wealth would be continued to lie fallow [uncultivated].

What does this author cite as negative effects of imperialism? _____

_____

What does he cite as positive effects of imperialism? _____

_____

(continued)

DBQ 18: Imperialism in Africa: An Evaluation(continued)

Document 5

This is an African proverb.

When the whites came to our country, we had the land and they had the Bible; now we have the Bible and they have the land.

What does this proverb imply about the effect of imperialism in Africa?_____
_____

Document 6

This poem by David Diop is from *An Anthology of West African Verse.*

The White Man killed my father,
My father was proud.
The White Man seduced my mother,
My mother was beautiful.
The White Man burnt my brother
beneath the noonday sun,

My brother was strong.
His hands red with black blood
The White Man turned to me;
And in the Conqueror's voice said,
"Boy! a chair, a napkin, a drink."

What negative aspects of imperialism does David Diop present in this poem? _____
_____

Document 7

This excerpt, adapted from *Balance Sheets of Imperialism* by Grover Clark, points out other negative aspects of imperialism.

The struggle for colonies does not result only in cash losses. There were also lives lost, wars fought, and hatreds aroused which threatened new wars. . . . Italy's trade with her colonies in 1894–1932 was worth 5,561 million lire [about $1,100 million]. This was less than one percent of her total foreign trade in the same period. In fact her expenditures on colonies for that time was 6,856 million lire. Obviously colonies cost more than they are worth in trade.

What evidence does this author provide to show that colonies were a negative financial drain on the Europeans? _____
_____

◆ **Part B—Essay**

Evaluate the new imperialism of the late nineteenth and early twentieth centuries in Africa. What were the positive and negative effects of imperialism for the colonizer and the colony?

Document-Based Assessment
Activities for Global History Classes

Grading Key

Document 1

Hobson points out the negative aspects of imperialism. There were many wars as the white races took over the territory of the "lower races" by force. The whites also took the most fertile land, the mines, and used the people for labor. The foreigners took the wealth out of the country.

Document 2

Toure believed that imperialism had a negative effect on Africans. They had no responsibility for their government and became convinced that they were inferior. As a result, their self-confidence was lacking.

Document 3

The All African People's Conference opposed imperialism in its declaration. They stated that imperialism should be condemned because it exploited African people and led to poverty in Africa. Also, the Africans had no freedom of speech, movement, worship, or association.

Document 4

This writer suggested that colonial people were not prepared for self-government and for running the industries of their countries. On the positive side, the Europeans provided the Africans with protection. The colonial powers also opened up the resources of Africa that the Africans lacked the money to develop. This author saw positive and negative effects for the colony.

Document 5

The proverb suggests that the Africans lost their land to the whites. The Africans got a new religion, Christianity, in return. It implies that the Africans lost more than they gained.

Document 6

This poem lists all that was taken from the African by the white man—lives, labor, and pride. The African was treated like a child.

Document 7

The author points out that imperialism was expensive for the colonizer. The European countries lost money and lives in the wars fought over colonial claims. These expenditures exceeded the trade benefits for European countries such as Italy.

Additional Information Beyond the Documents

The documents provide students with only fragments of evidence. Answers should include relevant information from beyond the documents—information that students have learned from their classroom study. The following list suggests some of the information that students might include in their essays from outside learning.

Maps of Africa
African conditions under European rule

Name_____ Date_____

DBQ 19: Causes of World War I

Historical Context:

At the turn of the twentieth century, Europe seemed to enjoy a period of peace and progress. Yet below the surface, several forces were at work that would lead Europe into the "Great War." One of these forces was nationalism, and it had an explosive effect in the Balkans. But, nationalism was only one of the many causes of World War I. Historians and eyewitnesses have described the causes of World War I and have tried to assess the responsibility for it. What were the causes of World War I?

◆ **Directions:** The following question is based on the accompanying documents in Part A. As you analyze the documents, take into account both the source of the document and the author's point of view. Be sure to:

1. Carefully read the document-based question. Consider what you already know about this topic. How would you answer the question if you had no documents to examine?

2. Now, read each document carefully, underlining key phrases and words that address the document-based question. You may also wish to use the margin to make brief notes. Answer the questions which follow each document.

3. Based on your own knowledge and on the information found in the documents, formulate a thesis that directly answers the question.

4. Organize supportive and relevant information into a brief outline.

5. Write a well-organized essay proving your thesis. The essay should be logically presented and should include information both from the documents and from your own knowledge outside of the documents.

Question: *Who and/or what caused World War I?*

◆ **Part A:** The following documents provide information on the causes of World War I. Examine the documents carefully, and answer the questions that follow.

Document 1

This chart provides information on the increasing amounts of money spent on armaments from 1870 through 1914.

Per Capita Expenditures of the Great Powers on Armaments						
	1870	**1880**	**1890**	**1900**	**1910**	**1914**
Great Britain	$3.54	$3.46	$3.84	$12.60*	$7.29	$8.23
France	2.92	4.02	4.66	5.21	6.47	7.07
Russia	1.28	1.50	1.26	1.44	2.32	3.44
Germany	1.28	2.16	2.80	4.06	4.06	8.19
Austria-Hungary	1.08	1.70	1.50	1.46	1.68	3.10
Italy	1.38	1.74	2.52	2.34	3.36	3.16

* Boer War Costs

Source: From *Europe, 1815–1914*, by Gordon A. Craig, 1966.

Which three countries increased the amount of money spent on weapons? _____

How did this increase the chance of war? _____

(continued)

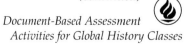

Document-Based Assessment
Activities for Global History Classes

DBQ 19: Causes of World War I *(continued)*

Document 2

This map of Europe on the eve of World War I shows the alliance systems.

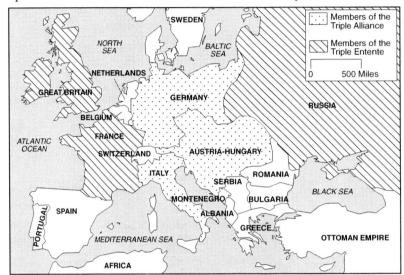

Who were the members of each alliance system? How did alliance systems contribute to the outbreak of World War I? _____

_____

_____

Document 3

This is an excerpt from the Austro-Hungarian Red Book No. 7. It is the ultimatum that Austria-Hungary sent to Serbia on July 23, 1914.

> . . . the Royal Serbian Government has done nothing to repress these movements. It has permitted the criminal machinations of various societies and associations directed against the Monarchy, and has tolerated unrestrained language on the part of the press, the glorification of the perpetrators of outrages and the participation of officers and functionaries in subversive agitation. . . .
>
> . . . [The] Royal Government see themselves compelled to demand from the Royal Serbian Government a formal assurance that they condemn this dangerous propaganda against the Monarchy. . . .
>
> . . . To accept the collaboration in Serbia of representatives of the Austro-Hungarian Government for the suppression of the subversive movement . . .

What were the accusations made by Austria-Hungary to Serbia? _____

_____

What two demands did Austria-Hungary make on Serbia? _____

_____

(continued)

DBQ 19: Causes of World War I *(continued)*

Document 4

This excerpt is from Article 231 of the Versailles Treaty, which Germany signed, thereby ending World War I.

> . . . The Allied and Associate Governments affirm and Germany accepts the responsibility of Germany and her allies for causing all the loss and damage. . . .

According to the Versailles Treaty, who was responsible for World War I? _____

Why? _____

Document 5

In this excerpt from May 7, 1919, Count Brockdorff-Rantzau, leader of the German delegation to the Versailles Peace Conference, protested.

> It is demanded of us that we shall confess ourselves to be alone guilty of the war. Such a confession from my lips would be a lie. We are far from declining all responsibility for the fact that this great World War took place or that it was fought in the way that it was. . . . But we energetically deny that Germany and its people, who were convinced that they fought a war of defense, were alone guilty. No one would want to assert that the disaster began only at that disastrous moment when the successor of Austria-Hungary fell a victim to murderous hands. In the last fifty years, the imperialism of all European states has chronically poisoned international relations. Policies of retaliation, policies of expansion, and disregard for the right of peoples to determine their own destiny, have contributed to the European malady which came to a crisis in the World War. The mobilization of Russia deprived statesmen of the opportunity of curing the disease, and placed the issue in the hands of the military powers. . . .

What position did the German delegation leader present? _____

_____

What did he say caused the war? _____

_____

Document 6

In his book, *Origins of the World War,* Sidney Bradshaw Fay stated his position on the causes of World War I.

> Nevertheless, a European war broke out. Why? Because in each country [of Europe] political and military leaders did certain things which lead to the mobilization [of their armies for war] and [finally] to the declarations of war, or [these leaders] failed to do certain things which might have prevented [the war]. In this sense, all the European countries in greater or lesser degree were responsible [for the outbreak of World War I].

(continued)

DBQ 19: Causes of World War I *(continued)*

According to this author, who was responsible for the outbreak of World War I? _____

_____

What did he cite as evidence to support this claim?_____

_____

_____

Document 7

This is an excerpt from *The Century of Total War* by Raymond Aron (Doubleday & Co. 1954).

. . . The rise of Germany, whose supremacy France dreaded and whose navy menaced [or threatened] England, had created among [England and France] an alliance which claimed it was defensive in nature but was denounced by German propaganda as an attempt at [the] encirclement [of Germany]. The two armed camps alarmed each other, and each grew heavy with multiplied incidents, which spread East [with the assassination of the Archduke Ferdinand], where Russia and Austria were advancing contradictory claims. . . .

What role did the assassination and the ultimatum play in the outbreak of the war? _____

_____

_____

What responsibility did the alliance systems play in the outbreak of the war? _____

_____

_____

◆ **Part B—Essay**

> *Who and/or what caused World War I?*

Grading Key

Document 1

According to this chart, Germany, Great Britain, and France spent the most per person on armaments. The money spent on armies and navies meant that these countries were prepared for war. This led to an arms race and fear among neighboring countries.

Document 2

The map shows that there were two alliance systems. The Triple Entente included Russia, France, and Great Britain. The Triple Alliance included Germany, Austria-Hungary, and Italy. The alliances produced two armed camps, ready for war.

Document 3

The Austrian ultimatum accused Serbia of doing nothing to control groups that were criticizing the Austrian monarchy. The Austrian government demanded that the Serbian government condemn the propaganda against Austria. Secondly, the Austro-Hungarian government said they would join with Serbia to investigate and suppress the "subversive" groups in Serbia.

Document 4

According to the Versailles Treaty, Germany accepted the blame. Germany lost the war and had to accept the terms given in the treaty.

Document 5

The leader of the German delegation said that Germany alone was not to blame. They were fighting a defensive war. He says the cause of the war was "imperialism of all European states." This imperialism led to conflict. When the Russians mobilized, military men took over and diplomacy faded.

Document 6

Fay believed all of the European countries were to blame for the war. The leaders either took steps that led to war, or did nothing to stop the war.

Document 7

Aron believed it was the alliance systems that brought on the war. Germany's rise in power threatened France and England who joined together in a defensive alliance. Germany saw itself encircled by enemies. Therefore, when the assassination occurred, the countries who already had conflicts were pulled into war.

Additional Information Beyond the Documents

The documents provide students with only fragments of evidence. Answers should include relevant information from beyond the documents—information that students have learned from their classroom study. The following list suggests some of the information that students might include in their essays from outside learning.

Nationalism among the subject nationalities in the Austro-Hungarian Empire and between European countries

Imperialism and economic rivalries among European nations

Alliance systems, militarism, the assassination of Archduke Francis Ferdinand, and the ultimatum

DBQ 20: Stalin: Evaluation of His Leadership

Historical Context:

Joseph Stalin is one of the most controversial leaders in world history. Between 1928 and 1941 he transformed the Soviet Union into a modern superpower. His rule is characterized by collectivized agriculture, rapid industrialization, great purges, and the extermination of opposition.

◆ **Directions:** The following question is based on the accompanying documents in Part A. As you analyze the documents, take into account both the source of the document and the author's point of view. Be sure to:

1. Carefully read the document-based question. Consider what you already know about this topic. How would you answer the question if you had no documents to examine?
2. Now, read each document carefully, underlining key phrases and words that address the document-based question. You may also wish to use the margin to make brief notes. Answer the questions which follow each document.
3. Based on your own knowledge and on the information found in the documents, formulate a thesis that directly answers the question.
4. Organize supportive and relevant information into a brief outline.
5. Write a well-organized essay proving your thesis. The essay should be logically presented and should include information both from the documents and from your own knowledge outside of the documents.

> **Question:** *Evaluate the rule of Stalin in the Soviet Union, taking into consideration the changes made and the methods used.*

◆ **Part A:** The following documents provide information about Stalin and the Soviet Union. Examine the documents carefully, and answer the questions that follow.

Document 1

Stalin launched his first Five-Year Plan in 1928 by setting up a planned, or command, economy. In this speech, Stalin arouses Russian pride to motivate the people.

> To slow down would mean falling behind. And those who fall behind are beaten. But we do not want to be beaten! One feature of the old Russia was the continual beatings she suffered for falling behind, for her backwardness. . . .
>
> Do you want our Socialist fatherland to be beaten? . . . If you don't want this, you must end our backwardness. You must develop a real Bolshevik tempo [speed] in building our Socialist economy. There is no other road.
>
> We lag behind the advanced countries by fifty to a hundred years. We must make good this distance in ten years. Either we do it, or we shall be crushed.

(continued)

DBQ 20: Stalin: Evaluation of His Leadership *(continued)*

What is Stalin trying to do in this speech? What method is he using to accomplish his goal?

_____

_____

_____

Document 2

When the first Five-Year Plan was announced in 1929, targets for industries were set that began rapid industrialization. (*Twentieth Century History*, Tony Howarth, Longman Group Ltd., 1979.)

Industry	1927–1928	Target for 1933
Electricity *(milliard kWh)*	5.05	17.0
Coal *(million tonnes)*	35.4	68.0
Oil *(million tonnes)*	11.7	19.0
Pig-iron *(million tonnes)*	3.3	8.0
Steel *(million tonnes)*	4.0	8.3

What is the goal of this Five-Year Plan? For what specific areas were goals set? _____

_____

_____

_____

Document 3

The following chart shows industrial production under the Five-Year Plans.

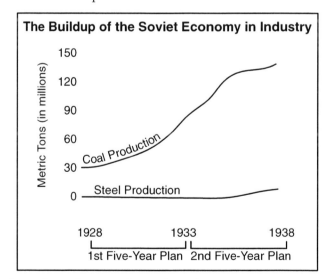

What does the chart show about Soviet industrial production? _____

_____

(continued)

DBQ 20: Stalin: Evaluation of His Leadership *(continued)*

Document 4

In this excerpt from a 1929 speech delivered by Stalin, he explains the collectivization policy and the need to eliminate the kulaks (wealthy farmers).

> The solution lies in enlarging the agricultural units . . . and in changing the agricultural base of our national economy. . . . the Socialist way, which is to set up collective farms and state farms which leads to the joining together of the small peasant farms into large collective farms, technically and scientifically equipped, and to the squeezing out of the capitalist elements from agriculture. . . . Now we are able to carry on a determined offensive against the kulaks, to break their resistance, to eliminate them as a class and substitute for their output the output of the collective farms and state farms.

According to Stalin, why and how must agricultural production be increased?_____

_____

_____

Why must the kulaks be eliminated? _____

_____

Document 5

The following illustrations show agricultural production during the First and Second Five-Year Plans.

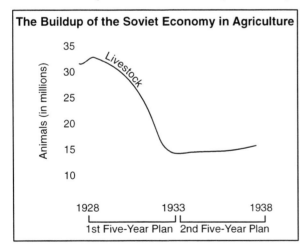

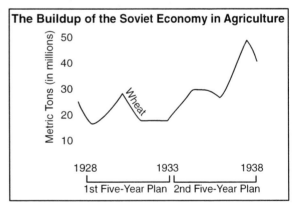

What do the charts show about livestock numbers and grain production? _____

_____

_____

_____

(continued)

DBQ 20: Stalin: Evaluation of His Leadership (continued)

Document 6

This excerpt, from "Forced Famine in the Ukraine: A Holocaust the West Forgot" by Adrian Karatnycky, was printed in *The Wall Street Journal*, on July 7, 1983.

> Today, reliable academic estimates place the number of Ukrainian victims of starvation at 4.5 million to 7 million. . . . The famine was in part the by-product of Stalin's relentless drive to collectivize Soviet agriculture. The famine was a clear result of the fact that between 1931 and 1933, while harvests were precipitously declining, Stalin's commissars continued to . . . confiscate grain. Peasants were shot and deported as rich, landowning "kulaks". . . . While the drive to collectivize agriculture was a wide-ranging phenomenon common to the entire U.S.S.R., only in the Ukraine did it assume a genocidal character. Indeed there can be no question that Stalin used the forced famine as part of a political strategy whose aim was to crush all vestiges of Ukrainian national sentiments.

According the this author, what were two explanations for the elimination of between 4.5 and 7 million Ukrainians between 1931 and 1933? _____

_____

_____

_____

Document 7

In contrast to prior documents, this excerpt from *The Land of Soviets*, published in the U.S.S.R., gives another perspective of the collectivization.

> The radical step forward by the majority of the peasantry towards a collective way of life was taking place against the backdrop of a bitter struggle between Soviet power and the kulaks. The [kulaks] stooped to all possible means to wreck the collectivization campaign. They murdered collective farm activists and Party and government officials sent to the villages to help the peasants; they set fire to collective farm buildings; they poisoned the cattle and destroyed farm machinery. . . . The Soviets had the right to banish them from their villages. . . . The exploiter class—the rural bourgeoisie—was finally abolished. . . .

In contrast, how does the Soviet author explain the actions taken against the kulaks? _____

_____

_____

_____

(continued)

Document-Based Assessment
Activities for Global History Classes

DBQ 20: Stalin: Evaluation of His Leadership *(continued)*

Document 8

This excerpt, from *The Land of the Soviets,* published in the U.S.S.R. describes the results of the Five-Year Plans.

> The fulfillment of the first and second Five-Year Plans strengthened the Soviet Union's economic position and turned it into a powerful industrial state. . . . In 1937 the industrial output of the USSR was 5.8 times larger than in 1913. The rate of industrial growth in the USSR considerably exceeded that of the capitalist countries. By 1937 the Soviet Union was the first country in Europe and the second in the world in the volume of industrial production. . . . Socialist industrialization was accompanied by the rapid growth of the working class, and made it possible to liquidate unemployment. In 1940 there were 9,971,000 industrial workers, which was nearly three times more than in 1928. The working class was also changing: its efficiency, technical and cultural levels were growing rapidly.

According to the Soviet author, what were the results of the Five-Year Plans? _____

_____

_____

_____

Document 9

In this excerpt, the French ambassador to the Soviet Union describes the public trials that were part of the "great purges" of Stalin.

> I personally attended the second and third Moscow trials, those of 1937 and 1938. . . . Pyatakov [another defendant] arose . . . confessed . . . to a number of crimes. Did these "confessions" carry any share of truth? It is possible that the accused were hostile to Stalin's regime. . . . But the lessons they recited must have been forced from them . . . it is more likely that the GPU [secret police] touched each at his weak point. It is also probable that the accused gave in to some form of pressure. . . . Some would give in to save their families, others in the hope of saving their own lives.

According to the French ambassador, what happened at the trials? _____

_____

_____

(continued)

DBQ 20: Stalin: Evaluation of His Leadership *(continued)*

Document 10

This Soviet poster was used to glorify Stalin.

Long live the great Stalin!

How did Stalin present himself in this poster? _____

_____

_____

◆ Part B—Essay

Evaluate the rule of Stalin in the Soviet Union, taking into consideration the changes made and the methods used.

Grading Key

Document 1

In this speech, Stalin reminded the Soviets that they had been beaten in the past due to their "backward-ness." Now, they needed to build up their economy very rapidly—in 10 years—or they would be crushed again. This speech was one of the methods Stalin used to motivate the Soviets to action.

Document 2

The first Five-Year Plan set up a command economy in which government planners set targets for industrial production and power supplies. The first column indicates what was actually produced in 1927–1928; the second column shows the goals the government wanted to achieve by 1933. In most cases, the target is twice as much or more for production in 1933, only five years hence. This would require great effort and sacrifice of consumer goods by the people and changes in the workplace as well as the workers. The method used by Stalin is state planning of a command economy and government control of the people's lives.

Document 3

The chart shows a dramatic increase in coal production between 1928 and 1938. There was also an increase in steel production. As a result, heavy industrial production increased.

Document 4

In this 1929 speech, Stalin explained how and why agriculture must change in order to feed the growing number of industrial workers. Farms would be joined together into state and collective farms, which would be equipped with the needed technology. As a result, food production would increase. But there was no room in this plan for the individual, capitalistic farmers, the kulaks. They must be driven out. Their agricultural production would be replaced with that of the state and collective farms. Thus Stalin was using the power of speech to motivate support for his economic plan and for the elimination of the kulaks as a class.

Document 5

These illustrations show the decline in livestock production. This was partly due to the government's policy against the kulaks. At the same time, wheat production generally increased.

Document 6

This author describes the famine that resulted as part of Stalin's collectivization of agriculture. Government officials continued to confiscate the grain of kulaks or peasants who resisted collectivization even though harvests were declining. Furthermore, the author claims that this government policy and the resulting "forced famine" was a genocide in the Ukraine. It was a political strategy used by Stalin to "crush all vestiges of Ukrainian national sentiments." It is a holocaust the West forgot, according to Karatnycky.

Document 7

This account from a Soviet perspective defends the actions taken by the Soviets against the kulaks. According to this Soviet account, the kulaks did everything they could to wreck the collectivization plan. They murdered government officials; they destroyed animals and farm machinery. Consequently the Soviets had the right to abolish the kulaks.

Document 8

This account from a Soviet perspective applauds the positive results of the Five-Year Plans. Industrial production was 5.8 times greater in 1937 than it was in 1913. In addition, unemployment was eliminated and the working class was more efficient and technically advanced. The Five-Year Plans turned the U.S.S.R. into a powerful industrial nation.

Document 9

This account describes the "great purges" that Stalin used to eliminate anyone he thought opposed him. These people confessed for a variety of reasons. This is a method used in totalitarian states to eliminate opposition.

Document 10

Posters and pictures were used by Stalin for his personal advancement. He attached himself to Lenin, the father of communism in Russia. In addition, he developed a cult of personality so that the Russians loved him as their father.

Additional Information Beyond the Documents

The documents provide students with only fragments of evidence. Answers should include relevant information from beyond the documents—information that students have learned from their classroom study. The following list suggests some of the information that students might include in their essays from outside learning.

Totalitarian government and their methods

Stalin and his practices in the U.S.S.R.

Conditions within Russia at the time

Changes made under Stalin

Sample Student Essay and Suggested Grading

Throughout history, people have pondered the role of Joseph Stalin, one of the most controversial leaders in world history. However, his rule can easily be proven both positive and negative for the country of Russia. Positively he made Russia into a military superpower. But his methods had a negative impact on Russia.

Among Stalin's accomplishments to the building of Russia, many were indeed positive. Stalin introduced a five-year economic plan, which gave a number of quotas for both industry and agriculture. "The fulfillment of the first and second Five-Year Plans strengthened the U.S.S.R.'s economic position . . ." *(Document 9)* As shown by charts illustrating both industrial and agricultural growth *(Documents 2, 3, 6)*, Stalin's economic venues helped Russia to become a modern industrial society and led to Russia's rise to a world power. Also the focus on heavy industry made to help increase the grandeur of the state. Under a command economy, in which the government controls all decisions made concerning the economy and personal lives, Russia with no doubt grew strong. Stalin said, "To slow down would mean falling behind. And those who fall behind are beaten. But we do not want to be beaten!" *(Document 1)* Attitudes such as these helped to rally the people of Russia, so that they came together as a united force. People came together to provide workers for the factories, and farmers on the collective farms. Stalin created a feeling of pride and nationalism that also helped this country grow strong.

Yet, for all of Stalin's positive accomplishments, he also seemed quite the negative ruler. First, Stalin developed a system of collective farming that combined once privately owned farms into large farms, operated by the government. This put an end to individual profits. Now he stressed, everything for the state must come first, the individual is second. "The Socialist ways set up collective farms . . . technically and scientifically equipped . . ., squeezing out of the capitalist elements from agriculture." *(Document 4)* Not only did he undermine the people of Russia, but he tortured, executed, or exiled anyone who opposed him. Continuing with the collective farming situation, kulaks, rich farmers disliked Stalin's system and openly resisted. Stalin immediately determined the kulaks should be punished. The kulaks were deported to forced labor camps or to Siberia. Stalin also used a forced famine in the Ukraine to torture, and control his people. ". . . in the Ukraine the collective farming assumed a genocidal character. . . . no question that Stalin used the . . . famine as a part of a political strategy . . ." *(Document 7)* In addition, in order to control his people, Stalin used propaganda to manipulate the people and provide only positive views of his communist dictatorship. In posters Stalin put himself in the shadows of Lenin, so as to be compared to a great leader, telling everyone that his methods were best for Russia. Stalin went as far as to use false trials to create and instill fear in his people. One French ambassador observed these trials and questioned, "Did these 'confessions' carry any share of the truth?" *(Document 10)* Stalin's radical means from these trials to his ". . . banish[ment]" of any opposition, truly created a terror-filled and negative image of Stalin.

In conclusion, although it is true that Stalin did much to positively affect the economy of Russia, he did so by harsh, cruel, and unneccesary means. He ultimately sacrificed his people, unmercifully for the outcome of the state.

Teacher Comments

This essay addresses all aspects of the task. It describes the changes made by Stalin, which made Russia into a superpower and industrial giant. It also describes the methods used by Stalin. It integrates outside information with information from the documents. The essay is well organized and has a strong introduction and conclusion. Score: level 5.

DBQ 21: World War II: The Road to War

Historical Context:

Even though the 1920's began with a favorable outlook for peace, toward the end of the decade and throughout the 1930's the clouds of war were forming. Dictators arose in countries that were dissatisfied with the results of World War I. Germany, Italy, and Japan took aggressive actions, and neither the League of Nations nor the democratic countries were able or willing to stop them. British Prime Minister Chamberlain suggested the best way to deal with Hitler was a policy of appeasement. Actions were taken that moved Europe toward war. The debate over the causes of World War II provides different perspectives.

◆ **Directions:** The following question is based on the accompanying documents in Part A. As you analyze the documents, take into account both the source of the document and the author's point of view. Be sure to:

1. Carefully read the document-based question. Consider what you already know about this topic. How would you answer the question if you had no documents to examine?

2. Now, read each document carefully, underlining key phrases and words that address the document-based question. You may also wish to use the margin to make brief notes. Answer the questions which follow each document.

3. Based on your own knowledge and on the information found in the documents, formulate a thesis that directly answers the question.

4. Organize supportive and relevant information into a brief outline.

5. Write a well-organized essay proving your thesis. The essay should be logically presented and should include information both from the documents and from your own knowledge outside of the documents.

> **Question:** *Why was the world plunged into World War II in 1939? What is the most effective response to aggression—appeasement or collective security?*

◆ **Part A:** The following documents provide information about the steps leading to World War II. Examine the documents carefully, and answer the questions that follow.

Document 1

In this excerpt from *Mein Kampf,* Adolf Hitler explains some of his ideas.

> One blood demands one Reich. Never will the German nation have the moral right to enter into colonial politics until, at least, it includes its own sons within a single state. . . . Oppressed territories are led back to the bosom of a common Reich, not by flaming protests, but by a mighty sword.

What does Hitler suggest is needed for Germany? How would that lead to war? _____

_____

_____

_____

(continued)

DBQ 21: World War II: The Road to War (continued)

Document 2

After Italy attacked Ethiopia, Haile Selassie, emperor of Ethiopia, asked the League of Nations for help in stopping the invasion. He asked for military sanctions but the League of Nations' response was ineffective. Haile Selassie used these words to the League of Nations:

> God and history will remember your judgement. . . . It is us today. It will be you tomorrow.

According to Haile Selassie, who should stop the aggressors? _____
_____

What will happen if the aggressors are not stopped? _____
_____

Document 3

Hitler promised to tear up the Versailles Treaty. Specifically, the treaty forbade German troops from entering the Rhineland, a buffer zone between Germany and France. The texts of two headlines and articles from *The New York Times* of March 8, 1936, explain this issue from the German and the French points of view.

HITLER SENDS GERMAN TROOPS INTO RHINELAND

Berlin, March 7—Germany today cast off the last shackles fastened upon her by the Treaty of Versailles when Adolf Hitler, as commander-in-chief of the Reich defense forces, sent his new battalions into the Rhineland's demilitarized zone. . . . "After three years of ceaseless battle," Hitler concluded, "I look upon this day as marking the close of the struggle for German equality status and with that re-won equality the path is now clear for Germany's return to European collective cooperation."

PARIS APPEALS TO LEAGUE

Paris, March 7—France has laid Germany's latest treaty violation before the Council of the League of Nations. At the same time the French Government made it quite clear that there could be no negotiation with Germany . . . as long as a single German soldier remained in the Rhineland in contravention [violation] of Germany's signed undertakings [agreements]. . . . What is essential, in the French view, is that the German government must be compelled by diplomatic pressure first and by stronger pressure if need be, to withdraw from the Rhineland.

What action did Hitler take in defiance of the Versailles Treaty? How does he explain his action?
_____
_____

What was the reaction in France? How might this have led to war? _____
_____

(continued)

DBQ 21: World War II: The Road to War (continued)

Document 4

As German aggression continued in 1938, Britain, France, and Italy met with Hitler to discuss his demands for the Sudetenland, a section of Czechoslovakia. This radio broadcast by William Shirer describes what happened at this meeting.

> **William Shirer:** It took the Big Four just five hours and twenty-five minutes here in Munich today to dispel the clouds of war and come to an agreement over the partition of Czechoslovakia. There is to be no European war . . . the price of that peace is . . . the ceding by Czechoslovakia of the Sudeten territory to Herr Hitler's Germany. The German Fuhrer gets what he wanted. . . . His waiting ten short days has saved Europe from a world war . . . most of the peoples of Europe are happy that they won't have to go marching off to war. . . . Probably only the Czechs . . . are not too happy. But there seems very little that they can do about it in face of all the might and power represented here.

What happened at this Munich Conference according to Shirer? What does he feel is the reaction in Europe and in Czechoslovakia? _____

_____

_____

_____

Document 5

In this speech to Parliament, British Primer Minister Neville Chamberlain explains why he favored a policy of appeasement in dealing with Hitler at Munich in 1938.

> With a little good will and determination, it is possible to remove grievances and clear away suspicion. . . . We must try to bring these four nations into friendly discussion. If they can settle their differences, we shall save the peace of Europe for a generation.
>
> And, in *The Times* (London): I shall not give up the hope of a peaceful solution. . . . We sympathize with a small nation faced by a big and powerful neighbor. But we cannot involve the whole British Empire in war simply on her account. If we have to fight, it must be on larger issues than that. . . . I am a man of peace. . . . Yet if I were sure that any nation had made up its mind to dominate the world by fear of its force, I should feel that it must be resisted. . . . But war is a fearful thing.

Why does Chamberlain suggest appeasement? _____

_____

_____

Under what conditions would he fight? _____

_____

_____

(continued)

DBQ 21: World War II: The Road to War *(continued)*

Document 6

Winston Churchill disagreed with Chamberlain's policy of appeasement. In this speech to Parliament, Churchill warned England about following a policy of appeasement.

> I have always held the view that keeping peace depends on holding back the aggressor. After Hitler's seizure of Austria in March, I appealed to the government. I asked that Britain, together with France and other powers, guarantee the security of Czechoslovakia. If that course had been followed, events would not have fallen into this disastrous state. . . . in time, Czechoslovakia will be swallowed by the Nazi regime. . . . I think of all the opportunities to stop the growth of Nazi power which have been thrown away. The responsibility must rest with those who have control of our political affairs. They neither prevented Germany from rearming, nor did they rearm us in time. They weakened the League of Nations. . . . Thus they left us in the hour of trial without a strong national defense or system of international security.

What strategy did Churchill suggest for keeping peace and stopping the growth of Nazi power?

_____

_____

In his opinion, what opportunities had been lost in the quest for peace?_____

_____

_____

Who is responsible for these lost opportunities? _____

_____

Document 7

In this excerpt from *Russia and the West Under Lenin and Stalin*, George F. Kennan offers another critical view of the Munich Agreement (Boston: Atlantic Little Brown, 1961).

> The Munich Agreement was a . . . desperate act of appeasement at the cost of the Czechoslovak state, performed by Chamberlain and French premier, Daladier, in the vain hope that it would satisfy Hitler's stormy ambition, and thus secure for Europe a peaceful future. We know today that is was unnecessary . . . because the Czech defenses were very strong . . . and because the German generals, conscious of Germany's relative weakness at that moment, were actually prepared to attempt to remove Hitler . . . had he continued to move toward war.

What are two reasons Kennan felt the Munich Agreement was unnecessary? _____

_____

_____

(continued)

DBQ 21: World War II: The Road to War *(continued)*

Document 8

In this excerpt adapted from British historian A. J. P. Taylor's *The Origins of the Second World War* (New York: Atheneum, 1965, p. 291), another point of view on appeasement is presented.

> Can any sane man suppose . . . that other countries could have intervened by armed force in 1933 to overthrow Hitler when he had come to power by constitutional means and was apparently supported by a large majority of the German people. The Germans put Hitler in power; they were the only ones who could turn him out. Also the "appeasers" feared that the defeat of Germany would be followed by a Russian domination over much of Europe.

What were two reasons this author used to explain why appeasement was the logical policy at

that time? _____

_____

_____

Document 9

In this excerpt by Keith Eubank from *Origins of World War II*, the author argues that the discussion about stopping Hitler prior to 1939 was not an issue for several reasons.

> . . . neither the people nor the government of [Britain and France] were conditioned to the idea of war. . . . Before September 1, 1939, Hitler had done nothing that any major power considered dangerous enough to warrant precipitating [starting] a major European war. Nor was there any existing coalition that could have opposed Hitler's massive forces. For Britain sought to appease Hitler [and] the French feared a repetition of the bloody sacrifices of 1914–1918. Stalin wanted an agreement with Hitler on partitioning Europe and the United States rejected all responsibility for Europe.

What evidence does this historian give for his belief that Hitler would not have been stopped

prior to 1939? _____

_____

_____

◆ **Part B—Essay**

> *Why was the world plunged into World War II in 1939? What is the most effective response to aggression—appeasement or collective security?*

Grading Key

Document 1

According to Hitler, Germany needed to unite all its people under one government—the Reich. It should be accomplished by force—"the sword."

Document 2

Haile Selassie wanted the League of Nations to stop Italian aggression. If the aggressor was not stopped, he would attack others. The aggressor should not be appeased.

Document 3

Hitler moved his troops into the Rhineland in violation of the Treaty of Versailles. He did this because he said it was time for Germany to be treated as an equal to the rest of the countries of Europe and no longer as a defeated punished nation. France went to the League of Nations and asked that Germany be removed from the Rhineland diplomatically or by "stronger pressure" if necessary.

Document 4

At the Munich Conference, the Big Four agreed to give the Sudetenland to Germany. According to Shirer, the Europeans were happy because war was avoided. The Czechs were not happy, but they couldn't resist in the face of the power present.

Document 5

Chamberlain suggested appeasement because he believed "good will and determination" could solve differences among countries peacefully. He said they could not fight to save Czechoslovakia because it is a small country. But he is willing to fight over big issues. Specifically, he says he will fight to stop a country that is using force to take over the world, but he does not want war and prefers diplomacy and appeasement.

Document 6

According to Churchill, the aggressor must be stopped. Britain, France, and the other countries must join together (collective security) to stop aggression. They should have stopped Hitler when he seized Austria and when he threatened Czechoslovakia, which he eventually took over. The responsibility for the "disastrous state" of England rests with the British government, which weakened the League of Nations and did not build up their defenses. In addition, the British government did not stop Germany from rebuilding her army. Appeasement does not work. It only postpones the inevitable conflict that will come.

Document 7

This author believed that appeasement was unnecessary because Czechoslovakia was strong enough to save herself. In addition, the German generals were about to overthrow Hitler.

Document 8

Historian Taylor defends appeasement. He said there was little basis for suggesting that the Germans would reject Hitler since they had put him in power and supported him. In addition, the other countries were worried about Russian expansion in Europe.

Document 9

The writer claims that the countries of Europe, especially Britain and France, were not willing to fight because Hitler had done nothing that would warrant their returning to the conditions they had suffered in World War I. All the countries had other interests and they were not willing to unite to stop Hitler. Collective security was not an option for them at that time.

Additional Information Beyond the Documents

The documents provide students with only fragments of evidence. Answers should include relevant information from beyond the documents—information that students have learned from their classroom study. The following list suggests some of the information that students might include in their essays from outside learning.

Causes of World War II—alliance system, hatred for the Versailles Treaty, weaknesses of the League of Nations (collective security)

Hitler's basic ideas about race, *lebensraum,* and Germany's rightful place in the world

DBQ 22: The Cold War Begins

Historical Context:

    Between 1945 and 1950, the wartime alliance between the United States and the Soviet Union broke down and the Cold War began. For the next 40 years, relations between the two superpowers swung between confrontation and détente. Each tried to increase its worldwide influence and spread its competing economic and political systems. At times during this period the competitors were at the brink of war. How was the Cold War fought?

◆ **Directions:** The following question is based on the accompanying documents in Part A. As you analyze the documents, take into account both the source of the document and the author's point of view. Be sure to:

    1. Carefully read the document-based question. Consider what you already know about this topic. How would you answer the question if you had no documents to examine?

    2. Now, read each document carefully, underlining key phrases and words that address the document-based question. You may also wish to use the margin to make brief notes. Answer the questions which follow each document.

    3. Based on your own knowledge and on the information found in the documents, formulate a thesis that directly answers the question.

    4. Organize supportive and relevant information into a brief outline.

    5. Write a well-organized essay proving your thesis. The essay should be logically presented and should include information both from the documents and from your own knowledge outside of the documents.

> **Question:** *How did the Cold War begin and what "weapons" were used to fight this war?*

◆ **Part A:** The following documents provide information about the Cold War. Examine the documents carefully, and answer the questions that follow.

Document 1

This is an excerpt from Winston Churchill's "Iron Curtain" speech, March 5, 1946.

> From Stettin in the Baltic to Trieste in the Adriatic, an iron curtain has descended across the continent. Behind that line lie all the capitals of the ancient states of Central and Eastern Europe. . . . All these famous cities and the populations around them lie in the Soviet sphere and all are subject in one form or another, not only to Soviet influence but to a very high and increasing measure of control from Moscow.

How is the "iron curtain" a dividing line? _____

_____

_____

_____

(continued)

*Document-Based Assessment
Activities for Global History Classes*

DBQ 22: The Cold War Begins *(continued)*

Document 2

This is an excerpt from President Truman's speech to Congress, March 12, 1947.

> I believe it must be the policy of the United States to support free peoples who are resisting attempted subjugation [domination] by armed minorities or by outside pressure. Should we fail to aid Greece and Turkey in this fateful hour, the effect will be far-reaching to the West. The seeds of totalitarian regimes are nurtured by misery and want. They spread and grow in the evil soil of poverty and strife. They reach their full growth when the hope of a people for a better life has died. Therefore, I propose giving Greece and Turkey $400 million in aid.

Explain the policy President Truman suggested in this speech. _____
_____

Document 3

This is an excerpt from Secretary of State Marshall's speech explaining his plan for European recovery, June 5, 1947.

> I need to say that the world situation is very serious. . . . Europe must have a great deal of additional help, or face heavy economic, social, and political damage. This would have a harmful effect on the world at large. There are also possibilities of disturbances because of the desperation of the people concerned. The effect on the economy of the United States should be clear to all. So the United States should do whatever it can to help restore normal economic health to the world. Without this there can be no political stability or peace. Our policy is directed . . . against hunger, poverty, desperation and chaos [disorder]. Its purpose is to revive a working economy in the world.

Why did Secretary of State Marshall suggest this plan for European recovery? _____
_____

Document 4

This is an excerpt from the North Atlantic Treaty, which was signed by the United States, Canada, and ten nations of Western Europe in 1948.

> The parties agree that an armed attack against one or more of them in Europe or in North America shall be considered as an attack against them all. They agree that if such an armed attack occurs, each of them will assist the party or parties so attacked. Each will immediately take whatever action it considers necessary to restore and maintain the security of the North Atlantic area. It will, if necessary, use armed force.

What is the purpose of NATO? _____
_____

(continued)

123   *Document-Based Assessment*
Activities for Global History Classes

DBQ 22: The Cold War Begins *(continued)*

Document 5

The Soviet Union responded to NATO by creating its alliance, the Warsaw Pact (shown below).

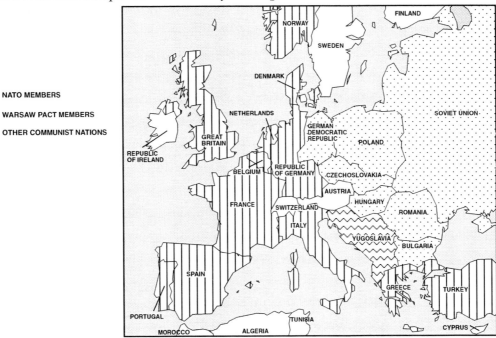

NATO MEMBERS

WARSAW PACT MEMBERS

OTHER COMMUNIST NATIONS

How do these "satellites" in the Warsaw Pact provide a buffer for the Soviet Union?_____

Document 6

This is an excerpt from a speech by Soviet Premier Nikita Khrushchev in 1956 in which he explains his point of view on U. S. actions.

> The inspirers of the "cold war" began to establish military blocs—the North Atlantic bloc, SEATO, and the Baghdad pact. [They claim] they have united for defense against the "communist threat." But this is sheer hypocrisy! We know from history that when planning a redivision of the world, the imperialist powers have always lined up military blocs. Today the "anti-communism" slogan is being used as a smoke screen to cover up the claims of one power for world domination. The United States wants, by means of blocs and pacts, to secure a dominant position in the capitalist world. The inspirers of the "position of strength" policy assert that it makes another way impossible because it ensures a "balance of power" in the world. [They] offer the arms race as their main recipe for the preservation of peace! It is perfectly obvious that when nations compete to increase their military might, the danger of war becomes greater, not lesser. Capitalism will find its grave in another world war, should it unleash it.

(continued)

DBQ 22: The Cold War Begins *(continued)*

What is Khrushchev's view of U.S. actions? According to Khrushchev what will happen?

_____

_____

_____

Document 7

The arms race was an important part of the Cold War. Both superpowers developed technology and used their nuclear power to build as many weapons as possible. This nuclear buildup led to a "balance of terror," which some saw as a deterrent to war. But others feared the use of these weapons. These charts show the build up of ICBM's and long-range bombers between 1966 and 1974.

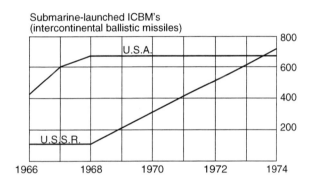

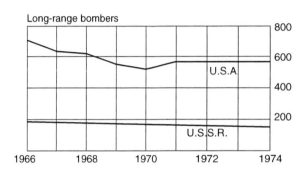

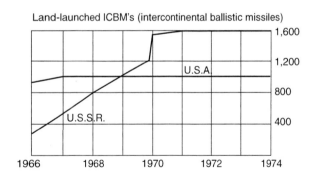

What impact did this arms race have on the world? _____

_____

_____

_____

(continued)

Document-Based Assessment
Activities for Global History Classes

DBQ 22: The Cold War Begins (continued)

Document 8

The threat of nuclear war was obvious in the Cuban missile crisis of 1962. This excerpt, from President John F. Kennedy's speech to the American people, explains the U.S. position.

> . . . We have unmistakable evidence that a series of offensive missile sites is now being built on that island. . . . Cuba has been made into an important strategic base by the presence of these long-range offensive weapons of sudden mass destruction. This is an open threat to the peace and security of all the Americas. Our objective must be to prevent the use of these missiles against this or any other country. We must secure their withdrawal from the Western Hemisphere. . . . I call upon Chairman Khrushchev to halt and eliminate this secret and reckless threat to world peace.

What is the basis for President Kennedy's demand that the missiles be removed from Cuba?

_____

_____

_____

Document 9

After Kennedy ordered a quarantine of all offensive military equipment being sent into Cuba, Premier Khrushchev responded with this message.

> Mr. President, the Soviet government decided to help Cuba with means of defense against outside attack. These weapons were only meant for defensive purposes. We have supplied them to prevent aggression against Cuba. . . . With respect and confidence I accept the statement you set forth in your message of October 27, 1962. You said then that Cuba will not be attacked or invaded by any country of the Western Hemisphere. . . . We have given the order to discontinue building the installations. We shall dismantle them and withdraw them to the Soviet Union.

How does Khrushchev explain why missiles were placed in Cuba and why they could now be

removed? _____

_____

_____

_____

◆ **Part B—Essay**

> *How did the Cold War begin and what "weapons" were used to fight this war?*

Grading Key

Document 1

Winston Churchill stated that an "iron curtain" or a great division exists between Eastern and Western Europe. The East European governments adopted a communist system and fell under the control of the U.S.S.R.

Document 2

President Truman proposed that the U.S. give $400 million in aid to Greece and Turkey to allow them to resist domination by outside pressure (Communists). This financial aid would remove the poverty and misery which plagued the countries after the war. As a result they would have hope for a better life and they would not turn to communism.

Document 3

In order to protect her interest and to restore "economic health" to the world, the U.S. needed to help rebuild Europe recover from the destruction suffered during the war. With U.S. aid the Europeans would not turn to communism and the U.S. would have trading partners.

Document 4

The North Atlantic Treaty joined the U.S., Canada, and ten European countries in a mutual defense pact. They would all be protected from Communist aggression. An armed attack on one would be considered as an armed attack on all.

Document 5

The U.S.S.R. responded with its defensive alliance for Eastern Europe. The Warsaw Pact countries, which were under Soviet control, served as a buffer between the U.S.S.R. and Western Europe.

Document 6

Khrushchev said the U.S. was setting up military blocs so that it could gain a dominant position in the capitalist world—not out of a fear of communism as the U.S. had said. In addition, the arms race was supposed to result in a balance of power. But according to Khrushchev, it could easily lead to war. Capitalism will end in "another world war" if it follows that path.

Document 7

The illustrations show the rapid build-up of ICBM's and long-range bombers. The lead in ICBM's was held by the U.S.S.R. in 1974. In contrast, the U.S. has more long-range bombers. The fear that either country might use these destructive nuclear weapons led to a balance of terror. This arms race led to dangerous competition between the two superpowers, which could have led to a nuclear war.

Document 8

In this speech, President Kennedy told the world about the nuclear threat that existed in Cuba. The offensive missiles could destroy most cities in the Western Hemisphere. Consequently, he demanded that the Soviet Union remove these missiles from Cuba and "end this dangerous arms race."

Document 9

Premier Khrushchev agreed to remove the missiles because he said they were only put there to defend and protect Cuba from an attack. Since the U.S. had promised that Cuba will not be attacked by any country in the Western Hemisphere, the missiles were no longer needed. The threat of nuclear war was lifted and the world stepped back from the brink of war.

Additional Information Beyond the Documents

The documents provide students with only fragments of evidence. Answers should include relevant information from beyond the documents—information that students have learned from their classroom study. The following list suggests some of the information that students might include in their essays from outside learning.

Competing ideological systems
Alliance systems
Arms race
Regional conflicts—Latin America, Vietnam, Korea, Berlin
Use of propaganda, economic and military aid to gain influence around the world
Containment, détente, and other policies of the U.S. and U.S.S.R.

DBQ 23: Decolonization and Revolution: 1945–1975

Historical Context:

Following World War II, there were major independence movements, as well as revolutions, to change the leadership of countries such as India, Vietnam, Cuba, China, and Ghana. Kwame Nkrumah said "This wind of change blowing through Africa . . . is a raging hurricane against which the old order cannot stand. . . . Thus we have witnessed the greatest awakening ever seen on the earth of suppressed and exploited peoples against the powers that have kept them in subjection. This, without a doubt, is the most significant happening of the twentieth century." At the same time in Cuba and China, Fidel Castro and Mao Zedong were leading revolutions to change their countries. Strong leaders shaped the movements for independence and change.

◆ **Directions:** The following question is based on the accompanying documents in Part A. As you analyze the documents, take into account both the source of the document and the author's point of view. Be sure to:

1. Carefully read the document-based question. Consider what you already know about this topic. How would you answer the question if you had no documents to examine?

2. Now, read each document carefully, underlining key phrases and words that address the document-based question. You may also wish to use the margin to make brief notes. Answer the questions which follow each document.

3. Based on your own knowledge and on the information found in the documents, formulate a thesis that directly answers the question.

4. Organize supportive and relevant information into a brief outline.

5. Write a well-organized essay proving your thesis. The essay should be logically presented and should include information both from the documents and from your own knowledge outside of the documents.

> **Question:** *Evaluate the methods and roles of leaders and organizations in the movement for independence and change in the period between 1945 and 1975.*

◆ **Part A:** The following documents provide information about revolutions and the independence movements that swept the world after World War II. Examine the documents carefully, and answer the questions that follow.

(continued)

DBQ 23: Decolonization and Revolution: 1945–1975 *(continued)*

Document 1

This excerpt, from the "Declaration Against Colonialism," was adopted by the United Nations in 1960.

The General Assembly,
   Mindful of the determination proclaimed by the peoples of the world in the Charter of the United Nations to reaffirm faith in fundamental human rights, in the dignity and worth of the human person . . . , Solemnly proclaims the necessity of bringing to a speedy and unconditional end colonialism in all its forms . . . And to this end Declares that:
1. The subjection of peoples to alien subjugation, domination and exploitation . . . is contrary to the Charter of the United Nations and is an impediment to the promotion of world peace and co-operation.
2. All peoples have the right to self-determination; by virtue of that right they freely determine their political status and freely pursue their economic, social and cultural development.

What is the main idea of this U.N. declaration? _____

_____

Document 2

The following is an excerpt from Ho Chi Minh, a Vietnamese nationalist.

The whole Vietnamese people, animated by a common purpose, are determined to fight to the bitter end against any attempt by the French colonialists to reconquer their country.

Describe the method Ho Chi Minh recommended to the Vietnamese people. _____

_____

Document 3

This excerpt, written by Mohandas Gandhi, describes his method for fighting for Indian independence.

Passive [nonviolent] resistance is a method of securing rights by personal suffering; it is the reverse of resistance by arms. . . . If I do not obey the law and accept the penalty for its breach [breaking] I use soul-force. It involves sacrifice of self.

In describing the Salt March, in which he used passive resistance, Gandhi said the following:

If the awakening of the people in the country is true and real, the salt law is as good as abolished. [raising a lump of salt] With this, I am shaking the foundations of the British Empire.

Describe the method recommended by Gandhi to the Indian people. _____

_____

(continued)

Name_____ Date_____

DBQ 23: Decolonization and Revolution: 1945–1975 *(continued)*

What was Gandhi's goal? _____
_____

Document 4

These are the words of Nelson Mandela as he fights for the end of apartheid in South Africa.

During my lifetime I have dedicated myself to the struggle of the African People. I have cherished the ideal of a democratic and free society in which all persons live together in harmony and with equal opportunities. It is an ideal which I hope to live for and to achieve. But, if needs be, it is an ideal for which I am prepared to die.

What change does Mandela recommend for South Africa? Explain. _____
_____

Document 5

Kwame Nkrumah, the leader in the fight for Ghana's independence, described the movement with these words:

Independence for the Gold Coast was my aim. It was a colony and I have always regarded colonialism as the policy by which a foreign power binds territories to herself by political ties, with the primary object of promoting her own economic advantage.

. . . Thus we have witnessed the greatest awakening ever seen on this earth of suppressed and exploited peoples against the powers that have kept them in subjection. This, without a doubt, is the most significant happening of the twentieth century.

What is the "most significant happening of the twentieth century" according to Nkrumah?
_____

Why is he opposed to colonialism? _____
_____

Document 6

Jomo Kenyatta, leader of the fight for independence for Kenya, and its first president, said the following.

The land is ours. When Europeans came, they kept us back and took our land. The freedom tree can only grow when you pour blood on it.

What is the reason for Kenyatta's call for independence? Explain. _____
_____
_____

(continued)

DBQ 23: Decolonization and Revolution: 1945–1975 *(continued)*

Document 7

This excerpt is from a speech given by Mao Zedong in 1945.

> Our aim . . . is to build up the confidence of the whole [Communist] Party and the entire people in the certain triumph of the revolution. . . . We must . . . raise the political conscious-ness of the entire people so that they may willingly and gladly fight together with us for victory. We should fire the whole people with the conviction that China belongs not to the reactionaries but to the Chinese people. . . . We firmly believe that, led by the Chinese Communist Party . . . the Chinese people will achieve complete victory. . . .

What is Mao Zedong attempting to do in this speech? _____

_____

Describe his method of change. _____

_____

Document 8

These are the words of Fidel Castro spoken in his defense at a trial in 1953.

> When we speak of struggle, the people means the vast unredeemed masses, to whom all make promises and who all deceive; we mean the people who yearn for a better, more digni-fied and more just nation . . . people who, to attain these changes, are ready to give even the very last breath of their lives—when they believe in something or in someone. . . .
>
> These are the people, the ones who know misfortune and, therefore, are capable of fighting with limitless courage! To the people whose desperate roads through life have been paved with the bricks of betrayal we . . . say . . . Here you have it, fight for it with all your might so that liberty and happiness may be yours.

Which "people" does Fidel Castro feel are the basis of the Cuban Revolution? _____

_____

_____

_____

_____

◆ **Part B—Essay**

> *Evaluate the methods and roles of leaders and organizations in the movement for indepen-dence and change in the period between 1945 and 1975.*

Grading Key

Document 1

The General Assembly of the United Nations in the "Declaration Against Colonialism" called for an end to colonialism. It is a fundamental human right for the people of a country to be free from control by another country. All people have the right to choose the government they want and to develop their own economy and culture. The U.N. encouraged all nations to work together and to strive for world peace.

Document 2

Ho Chi Minh, the nationalist leader who fought for Vietnamese independence from the French, urged the Vietnamese people to unite and fight to the end to prevent the French from regaining control. He is an inspiration to the people as he dedicated his life to the goal of independence.

Document 3

Gandhi, in leading the fight for India's independence from Great Britain, urged the use of passive resistance. He would not obey unjust laws and was ready to accept the consequences. He used this method in the salt march. He felt that if the Indian people refused to pay the salt tax, the British Empire would start to break up. India would gain independence by passive resistance. India would use peaceful means—"soul force."

Document 4

Mandela, in his fight to end apartheid, was willing to die for his goal: that all people live together in a "democratic and free" society. It would mean the end of apartheid, which had separated and subjugated the blacks in South Africa.

Document 5

Nkrumah, in his fight for independence for the Gold Coast (Ghana), felt the independence movement that was sweeping Africa was the most important event in the twentieth century. This movement would sweep away colonialism. Nkrumah was against colonialism because he said its primary purpose was to gain wealth for the foreign power.

Document 6

Kenyatta claimed that the Europeans had taken the land that belongs to the people of Kenya, who must be willing to shed their blood to regain their independence. Kenyatta was motivating the people to fight.

Document 7

Mao Zedong made the Chinese people aware of the need to fight together against the "reactionaries" (the Nationalists). Mao was raising the confidence of and predicting a victory for the Chinese people if they followed the leadership of the Communist party.

Document 8

In this speech, Castro is rallying the support of the Cuban people to fight against the dictator. The people are the masses who want a better, more just country. The people must be willing to die for what they believe in. The people for whom he is fighting are the unemployed, the laborers, small businessmen, and young professionals who are not doing well under the dictator's regime. They must fight for liberty and happiness. It is their duty to be revolutionaries.

Additional Information Beyond the Documents

The documents provide students with only fragments of evidence. Answers should include relevant information from beyond the documents—information that students have learned from their classroom study. The following list suggests some of the information that students might include in their essays from outside learning.

Information about independence movements and methods
Leaders for independence—Mandela, Ho Chi Minh, Gandhi, Kenyatta, Nkrumah
Revolutionary leaders—Fidel Castro for the Cuban Revolution and Mao Zedong for the Chinese Revolution of 1949
Methods used to motivate and fight for change and independence